WHAT ~~PEOPLE ARE~~
SAYING

Linda Acker is passionate about her love for the Lord and His Word and her desire to help others grow in faith. Her talent for describing an everyday situation and progressing to a spiritual concept brings the reader fact to fact with God's truth, plus the opportunity for personal application. I highly recommend this book! You will be blessed.

Fran Caffey Sandin, author of *Hope on the Way: Devotions to Go,*
See You Later, Jeffrey, and *Touching the Clouds*
Member of Advanced Writers and Speakers Association, and friend

Linda weaves relatable everyday observations and occurrences with profound biblical truths, making these devotionals accessible to every reader. Her joy in the Lord and zest for life are palpable through the written word. If you are reading *Seeing God in the Ordinary Things*, rest assured she has prayed blessings over you.

Kalina Collier, Women's Ministry Leader at Ridgecrest Church,
Greenville, Texas, and friend

This collection of devotions, taken from everyday life experiences, is a compelling invitation for all of us to look for God as we traverse each day. Linda teaches us to recognize God's presence in ordinary experiences and adventures. She has chosen to rejoice as she travels this earthly realm, and her stories reflect her delight in the Lord.

Becky McConnell, Bible study teacher at FBC Forney, Texas,
and Linda's little sister

I love how Linda uses everyday experiences to speak to my heart and guide me into a deeper understanding and relationship with God. Her unique crafting of words makes a sweet melody that is easy to read while shouting profound truth from scripture.

Siri Livengood, Apples of God teacher,
Community Bible Study Leader and friend

Linda has a delightful way of connecting the ordinary realities of life to deep spiritual truths. As self-examination follows, a heart can't help but be drawn by the Holy Spirit to fall more in love with Jesus and His goodness.

Corrie Petzgold, Zone Director for Community Bible Study, Discipleship Coordinator for Women's Ministry at Ridgecrest Baptist Church, and friend

In her book, *Seeing God in the Ordinary Things*, Linda uses personal experiences and insights to point us toward the God of every day. She challenges us not only to see God all around us but also to go deeper and further in our understanding and desire to be more like Him. I believe Linda's words will uplift, inspire, and challenge every reader.

Joel Bench, Pastor of Discipleship, Ridgecrest Baptist Church, Greenville, TX

Cover and Interior Layout @ 2023 Harvest Creek Publishing and Design
www.harvestcreek.net   info@harvestcreek.net

Ordering Information: Special discounts are available on quantity purchases by churches, associations, and others. For details, please contact the author at lgacker@aol.com.

Seeing God in the Ordinary Things—1st edition

ISBN: 978-1-961641-09-9

Printed in The United States of America

CONTENTS

FOREWORD

In their book, *Move: What 1,000 Churches Reveal About Spiritual Growth,* Greg L. Hawkins and Cally Parkinson presented the findings of an in-depth study of 1,000 churches and over 250,000 congregants. The authors claimed that the interpretation of the data revealed discernable stages of spiritual growth as well as various catalysts for growth between each stage—beliefs and activities that propel one through across the continuum of spiritual growth.

One activity stood out. One practice stood out in terms of how it influenced our growth from stage to stage. The authors called this practice the "vanilla factor" of spiritual growth. Vanilla ice cream is, by far, the most popular flavor, twice as popular as the runner-up, chocolate. And chocolate is twice as popular as any other flavor. So, vanilla stands heads and shoulders above other flavors as the most popular ice cream flavor.

One practice stands head and shoulders above all other beliefs, attitudes, and activities in its effect on our spiritual growth—reflecting on Scripture and its meaning in our lives. If we want to grow in our relationship with Christ, there is nothing better we can do than prayerfully meditate on the word of God and how it applies to our lives.

Linda Acker has a gift in her ability to internalize concepts she receives from the Bible, visualize them through her daily life, and communicate them in a palatable and digestible way for her readers. We find ourselves walking down her neighborhood road with her, noticing the leaves, and suddenly, we are also face to face with the gravity of our own choices to lead our daily struggles into joy as the

Spirit calls us to in the book of James. We join her in her joy of celebrating the playfulness of her grandchildren, and immediately, she reminds us of God's great love and faithfulness to us. As Scripture teaches in Deuteronomy, John, the Psalms, Isaiah, and elsewhere, she reminds us we need not live in fear.

In *Seeing God in the Ordinary Things*, Linda Acker invites us into her practice of the vanilla factor of spiritual growth. We are given a window into a heart that has made it a practice of reflecting on the truths of Scripture in everyday life. As we gaze through that window, we get a taste of one person's reflection on God's word and are encouraged and instructed. We also develop a taste for how we might reflect on Scripture from within our own daily lives. And just like vanilla ice cream, it tastes sweet!

—**Dr. Nick Acker**, Pastor at Grace Church in Ventura, California, and Linda's son

Make me to know your ways, O LORD;
Teach me your paths.
Lead me in your truth
and teach me,
For you are the God
of my salvation;
For you, I wait
all the day long.

PSALM 25:4-5 ESV

AMAZING GRACE

TODAY'S SCRIPTURE REFERENCE:

And from His fullness we have all received,
and grace for grace.
John 1:16 NKJV

The hummingbirds are here, and Glenn and I have put up three feeders. At least fifteen birds are zipping in and out, hovering here and there and everywhere! I say "at least" because they move so fast it is impossible to count the little boogers!

We enjoy watching their antics as they fuss and fight over who has dominion over a particular feeder. A bully always seems so afraid there will not be enough sweet water for him, much less everyone else! But here's the deal—Glenn and I ensure the sugar water will never run out. The tap water is always there, and the grocery store has not run out of sugar yet! *If only they knew.*

We're not all that different from these fussy birds, are we? We run about attempting to fix this or that, afraid we can't meet this or that deadline. The stress of paying bills and meeting others' needs weighs on us, leaving us feeling depleted and concerned about having enough. We worry there is insufficient time, energy, money, love, forgiveness, etc.

And all the while, our Heavenly Father watches with a pitcher full of "enough." He whispers confidently to our hearts, "My grace is sufficient for you. I will never leave you nor forsake you."

John 1:16 reminds us we have already received and will continue to receive grace piled up on top of grace, one blessing upon another! His grace supply never runs out—never!

> *And God is able to make all grace abound to you, so that*
> *having all sufficiency in all things at all times, you may*
> *abound in every good work.*
> 2 Corinthians 9:8 ESV

Although I don't understand grace completely, I know God gives as much as we need, exactly when we need it. I do not deserve it, but He freely gives it out of His love for me and His Son's sacrifice. So, my response will be one of thankful acceptance and worship.

Let's not be like the hummingbirds, flitting about in worry and fear. Instead, choose to rest in God's all-sufficient, extraordinary, amazing grace that springs from a well that never runs dry!

PRAYERFUL RESPONSE:

Take a moment to remember times when God poured out His grace on you. Spend some time thanking Him for His grace, asking Him to help you be more aware of its presence and impact on your life.

_____

_____

_____

_____

_____

_____

_____

_____

How can you extend grace to others?

_____

_____

_____

_____

_____

_____

_____

_____

ARMOR OF GOD

TODAY'S SCRIPTURE REFERENCE:

Pray at all times in the Spirit with every prayer and request,
and stay alert with all perseverance and
intercession for all the saints.
Ephesians 6:18 CSB

A couple of years ago, our Wednesday night Bible Study completed the book *The Armor of God,* written by Priscilla Shirer. Her study helped us understand and apply the armor of God described in Ephesians 6. One impactful lesson she taught is that there are *seven* pieces of armor, not six. Besides the belt of truth, the breastplate of righteousness, gospel shoes, the shield of faith, the helmet of salvation, and the sword of the Spirit, prayer is the last component.

As part of the study, they instructed us to write out prayers concerning each piece of armor. Listed below are my prayers, some of which are very personal but may help in your understanding of the armor of God.

Ephesians 6:14 - Father, Your Word is Truth; It is Who You are and who You say I am in You. O Father! Help me gird up my feelings, thoughts, and actions into Your Truth so that Your Truth would take all my thoughts captive (especially my feelings!).

Help me recognize when Satan is trying to use my thoughts and feelings to stir up anger and hurt in my relationships and help me to "slam the door" on those immediately before they have time to fester and grow.

Your truth strengthens me. Thank You, Father! When I face a challenge, I have Your full weight and the wind of the Holy Spirit reverberating behind me, holding me up and empowering me!

Ephesians 6:16 - Father, help me be still and KNOW that You are God! You are the Great I AM, the Faithful God, The God Who Sees, the Alpha and Omega, Almighty God, Prince of Peace! Help me see that faith is all about You, and rest in knowing who You are and who You say I am.

You've got all of "this," and You've got me. Thank You for Your sovereignty and your love. Help me keep my eyes on You. Strengthen my arm to wield these truths when those fiery arrows fly at me. I am sure He who began a good work in me will be faithful to complete it!

Ephesians 6:17 - Father, help me guard my mind, will, emotions, and conscience. Show me quickly anytime my mind focuses on falsehoods or when my emotions are "out of whack" with Truth!

Oh, Father, thank You for the Cross! Please help me be mindful of all that it means. I am forgiven, and the penalty for my sins has been paid. Jesus' righteousness has been imputed to me! Thank You, Jesus, for so great a salvation!

Ephesians 6:10-18 - Father, help me totally depend on Your Word as my guide for my life—to walk in it, abide in it, and order my steps and decisions according to it! Keep my ears open to hear You say, "This is the way: walk in it."

Help me believe and act on Your truth. The Light of Your Word dispels the darkness and warms my heart. Take away the exposed fear and the lies that produce the fear, anger, bitterness, or hurt.

Praise You, Father, for giving us Your truth and for Being Truth to us and for us. Thank You for Your Great and Powerful Love!

In Jesus' Name, Amen

PRAYERFUL RESPONSE:

Write your *Armor of God* prayer.

_____

_____

_____

_____

_____

_____

_____

_____

BE THE LIGHT

TODAY'S SCRIPTURE REFERENCE:

In the beginning, God created the heavens and the earth.
Now the earth was formless and empty, darkness covered the
surface of the watery depths, and the Spirit of God was
hovering over the surface of the waters. Then God said, "Let
there be light," and there was light. ***God saw that the light***
was good, and God separated the light from the
darkness.
Genesis 1:1-4 CSB [Emphasis added]

When our boys were little, we took them to Meramec Caverns in Missouri. The caves were once the hideout of Jesse James and his riders, so that fact of history gave the boys an extra incentive to visit them. What we found inside was beautiful and unique. The rock formations included stalagmites and an amazing "stage curtain," a grand limestone wall shaped like a flowing curtain.

It was here at the curtain that our guide gave a demonstration. He turned out all the lights in that section, completely covering us in darkness. It was so dark that you could not see your hand in front of your face. We felt a sense of unease as darkness surrounded us entirely.

Then the guide took out his lighter and flicked it on. What a difference one tiny twinkle of light made in that utter darkness! Of course, the darkness hovered around us, but that small light made us feel safe again and less fearful of what might lurk in the darkness we could see!

In His first words to us, God revealed the truth that light dispels darkness; light overcomes darkness. John opens his gospel with, "In the beginning was the Word, and the Word was with God, and the Word was God. He was with God in the beginning. All things were created through Him, and apart from Him, not one thing was created that has been created. **In Him was life, and that life was the light of men. That light shines in the darkness, and yet the darkness did not overcome it**" (John 1:1-5 CSB Emphasis added). In the beginning . . . Jesus. He is the Light showing us the way to the Father.

When I go down to the dock after it starts to get dark, I always take a flashlight with me. Having encountered a snake more than once, I do not want that to happen again! Not only does that flashlight guide my steps, but it alerts me to what is around me, good or bad. When we believe that Jesus came to save us from the penalty of our sin and follow Him as His disciples, God reveals to us His mystery that Christ is in us, the Hope of glory; He shines in and through us. (Colossians 2:27)

In the Sermon on the Mount, Jesus, who is The Light, commands those who believe to be the Light. We are to let our light shine so that the world may see Him reflected in us and see Him. He enables us to do that by placing His own Spirit within us (2 Corinthians 1:22). Jesus told His disciples that the Counselor would come, The Spirit of truth, and He would testify of Jesus (John 15:26). The Holy Spirit teaches us and gives us wisdom into spiritual truths. (1 Corinthians 2:13) We also see in 2 Corinthians 3:6 CSB that Jesus "made us competent to be ministers of a new covenant, not of the letter, but of the Spirit."

How do we reflect the Light of Jesus to the world? First, we must abide in Him; He tells us in John that apart from Him, we can do nothing. We yield our wills to Him and rest in the truth that His Spirit is in us, working in us, with us, and through us to make us more like Christ in how we love and interact with the world around us.

Next, we carefully study Jesus' life in His Word. We learn from His examples of how to love others, build a life that honors the Father, build godly relationships with people, and grow deeper in love with Him so that His desires become our own. We listen and act upon words of truth revealed about Christ-like behaviors from the gospel writers.

Finally, we stand. We stand on our "hills," firmly committed to letting our lights shine in a world shrouded in darkness. We are watchful and alert in our armor of truth, righteousness, peace, salvation, faith, His Word, and prayer. (Eph. 6:13-18)

I don't know how God has called you to shine His Light into the world; we have our own calling in the places we are and where He sends us. Our job is to rest in Him and be in Him. Let Him be in you, knowing that He who began a good work will be faithful to complete it and shine His Light through us—the Light that became flesh and came into the world.

PRAYERFUL RESPONSE:

How will your light shine today in the darkness that hovers around us? Simply by walking in the light, your life will dispel whatever darkness you encounter as you reflect Jesus. What will you do or say today to help someone in the dark to see?

_____

_____

_____

_____

_____

_____

_____

_____

BIRDS OF A FEATHER

TODAY'S SCRIPTURE REFERENCE:

*Dear friend, do not imitate what is evil but what is good. The
one who does good is of God;
the one who does evil has not seen God.*

3 John 1:11 CSB

My mother and daddy were avid birdwatchers. Their passion for this pastime began when they were serving at Zephyr Baptist Encampment in south Texas. God called Daddy to be the camp manager when he was in his fifties. He and Mother served there for close to twenty years. It came as no surprise to us kids when he gave us bird books for identifying the birds in our backyards. Daddy also wrote a couple of bird books and a column in the local newspaper, *Birding with Bosie*.

All that to say, I have grown to love watching birds, too. On my walks down our country lanes, I enjoy watching them flit in and out of the trees. Their songs are a delight to listen to, reminding me of the beauty of God's creation.

Today, as a blue jay flew right past me and settled in a tree nearby, I had an epiphany: What kind of bird am I? I dared to hope I was NOT like a blue jay!

Blue jays are beautiful on the outside, but I have observed how mean they are to the other birds! I thought about the passage in James where he discusses the dangers of an "unruly tongue." In chapter three, he compares our words to fire out of control. In verses 9-10 CSB, James states: "With the tongue, we bless our Lord and Father, and with it we curse people who are made in God's likeness. Blessing and cursing come out of the same mouth. My brothers and sisters, these things should not be this way."

In the book of Romans, Paul talks about our mouths speaking deceit, poison, cursing, and bitterness. Those who do so do not have the fear of God and do not know peace! I know you want to love God and people just like He does. Let's choose our words carefully so they reflect His character in us.

A bluebird family lives in one of our birdhouses; I think I would prefer to be like these birds. They are so pretty and are often referred to as "birds of happiness." One of my favorite passages in the Bible is Habakkuk 3:17-19 CSB, "Though the fig tree does not bud and there is no fruit on the vines, though the olive crop fails and the fields produce no food, though the flocks disappear from the pen and there are no herds in the stalls, YET I will celebrate in the LORD; I will rejoice in the God of my salvation! The LORD my Lord is my strength; he makes my feet like those of a deer and enables me to walk on mountain heights!"

My prayer is to always remember my God and my purpose in Him, even when facing adversity, for He grants me strength and guides me through dangerous places. As we navigate the craggy mountain trails, I pray to always remember that He is by my side, holding my hand.

My admiration for hawks grew when I saw one flying away from my yard with a snake hanging from its beak! I know he is a *predator*, but I saw him as a *protector*. That hawk sits alert and watchful at the tiptop of the trees, keenly watching the world around him. My goal is to embody the same alertness and self-control, fully aware of the devil's prowling nature, intent on sabotaging my witness (1 Peter 5:7).

Paul instructs us in 1 Corinthians 5:58 to stand firm and to let nothing move us, knowing that our labor in the Lord is not in vain. As a "hawk," we have the privilege and obligation to labor in prayer for our family and friends. As we put on God's armor, we are to saturate every piece with prayer, standing in the gap as watchful prayer warriors (Eph. 6:18)

And what about the cardinals? Aren't they beautiful? Their bright red feathers stand out, especially in the winter. We don't get much snow in Texas, but I've seen pictures of cardinals in the snow and am awed by their colorful display.

Does your life and mine stand out in this world? We are called to be holy as He is holy. Our lives should look very different from the rest of the world; Jesus said we are the light of the world! Because we belong to the Light, we should reflect the same self-control, love, and grace of our Savior, thus honoring Him and the gospel.

Were you aware that doves stay together as mates for their entire lives? In nature, we see an example of God's faithfulness and love. Our motivation to be faithful to God stems from His perfect faithfulness to us. He has promised that He will never leave us and that even in our faithlessness, He remains faithful to us; after all, Jesus is the Author and Perfector of our faith!

The last bird I will mention is one we do not want to imitate! The cuckoo is so selfish that they lay their eggs in the nests of other birds. It seems that they would rather spend their time flitting their lives away than doing the work of building a nest and caring for their own young. Rather than being so self-centered, we have been called to be living sacrifices, holy and pleasing to God . . .renewing our minds with His Word as He transforms us into His own image (Romans 12:1-2).

So, what specific bird are you? If we are honest with ourselves, we recognize some of each in how we live our lives. But, praise God, He has given us His Spirit, gently reminding us of who God is and what He is doing in us. Thankfully, He taps us on the shoulder when we are blue jays or cuckoos. Through His strength, we are granted the freedom to choose and the grace to fail. He is always there to help us "fly right"!

PRAYERFUL RESPONSE:

Describe how the characteristics of the blue jay, bluebird, hawk, dove, cuckoo, and cardinal are demonstrated in your life.

_____

_____

_____

_____

_____

_____

_____

_____

BUT JESUS . . .

TODAY'S SCRIPTURE REFERENCE:

*And I am sure of this, that he who began a good work in you
will bring it to completion at the day of Jesus Christ.*

Philippians 1:6 ESV

In studying the Bible inductively, I have learned to look for repeated words in a passage. Repeated words give insight into the writer's heart and what they are trying to convey through the Holy Spirit to the reader's heart. Once, while reading a passage in Luke, I noticed a little conjunction kept popping up. *But!* And this brief word was always followed by *Jesus* or by *He*. But Jesus.

So, I circled the word "but" every time it came up while reading the narrative. Without fail, whenever the writer mentioned "but Jesus" or "but He," something remarkable happened next! You can expect the unexpected when you discover a "but Jesus" in your Bible reading!

This realization got me thinking (*a scary thought, I know!*) How many "But Jesus" moments are there in my life? And am I grateful for them?

The principal thing is that as a sinner, I deserve hell and to pay for my sins. But Jesus—through His death and resurrection—paid my debt in full. My debt is canceled; I am forgiven, and I will spend eternity in heaven with Him. My gratitude for that alone should be over the moon!

Life has challenging moments. But Jesus promised that during those times, He would be with us—walking us through them and loving us.

I have been afraid. But Jesus has calmed my fears with His Word and His presence. I have been heartbroken. But Jesus has cried with me. He has comforted me and loved on me through friends and family, His Word, and Himself. I have been blessed with spiritual blessings. But Jesus continues to grow me in those blessings, His grace, mercy, and forgiveness, teaching me to love as He loves.

I fail often, but Jesus keeps teaching me truths like Philippians 1:6. I still sin. But Jesus, rich in mercy, faithful to forgive, and loving me with "crazy love," is always with me, disciplining me to make me more like Him.

This is my shortlist, as there is no room here for a longer one. The words "But Jesus" give us much for which to be grateful, don't they? Those words provide gratitude for His Grace in our lives and make us joyful, radiant people, thus eclipsing bitterness and complaining! Remember that the little conjunction "but" and the mighty name "Jesus" give us cause to worship! Let's gratefully remember all the "But Jesus" times in our lives!

PRAYERFUL RESPONSE:

Make a list of the "But Jesus" moments in your life.

_____

_____

_____

_____

_____

_____

_____

_____

_____

CALLED

TODAY'S SCRIPTURE REFERENCE:

With this in mind, we constantly pray for you, that our God may make you worthy of his calling, and that by his power he may bring to fruition your every desire for goodness and your every deed prompted by faith.

2 Thessalonians 1:11 NIV

When our son, Nick, moved his family to California to be pastor of Grace Church in Ventura, several catastrophic events happened within a few short months. First, they experienced an earthquake, a "shaking" event for a Texas family. Then there was a wildfire! It was so close to the church and parsonage that they could see it through their kitchen window. Of course, they were evacuated.

Next came the rains, bringing mudslides because of the fire. Following that came the plague of fleas. (Yuck!) The kids brought fleas into the house after playing with the dog left by the previous pastor.

If that wasn't enough, they heard scratching in the attic and discovered the house was infested with rats—big rats! It took many visits and traps from the exterminator to rid themselves of those pests. What a series of events!

My husband informed Nick that he believed God was summoning them back to Texas, using plagues similar to those used by Moses to convince Pharaoh to release His people. But Nick laughed and said, "No, Dad. God called us to California for His plans and purposes."

As I write about their initial months in California, I can't help but smile. But they loved their new church family and were well-loved by them throughout all their ordeals. Nick's words about God's calling on his life made me think about His calling on mine and yours. According to Peter, we are all called according to His promise, "chosen according to the foreknowledge of God the Father, through the sanctifying work of the Spirit, for obedience to Jesus Christ" (1 Peter 1:2 NIV).

I came up with a short list of the callings on our lives, individually and corporately:

- We are called to Salvation. 2 Timothy 1:9 says that God has saved us and called us to a holy life not because of anything we say or do but because of His own purpose and grace.
- We are called to be saints; Paul tells us this in Romans 1:7. Saints are those who have been set apart, sanctified, and consecrated to God, sharing in His purity and abstaining from earth's defilement.
- We are called to be the temple of God. "Do you not know that your body is a temple of the Holy Spirit, who is in you, whom you have received from God? You are not your own; you were bought with a price. Therefore, honor God with your body." (2 Corinthians 6:19-20)
- We are called to be ambassadors for Christ, sharing the gospel and representing Jesus to the world. (2 Corinthians 5:20)

- We are called to be holy, to walk in His righteousness with right living. (1 Corinthians 1:2)
- We are called to live in peace. Peace is one of the gifts of His Spirit (Galatians 5). Jesus Himself is our peace and brings us to peace with God and one another. (Ephesians 2:14-18)
- We are called to live in the freedom of grace. Romans 8:1 tells us that we no longer live in condemnation because Jesus set us free. Galatians 5:13 reminds us that we are called to be free to serve in love.
- We are called to one Hope. Paul prayed that believers would know the hope to which God called them, the "riches of His glorious inheritance in the saints, and His incomparably great power for us who believe." (Ephesians 1:18-19)
- We are called to have the mind of Christ...to think and meditate on His words and actions until they become part of us... of how we react to and love Him and others. (Romans 12:1-2)
- We are called to be a blessing to others. (1 Peter 3:9)
- We are called to love one another. (1 John 4:7)
- We are called to have thankful hearts. "Rejoice in the Lord always . . . by prayer and petition, with thanksgiving, present your requests to God." (Philippians 4: 4-6)

There are many other callings on our lives; some will be specific to each person wherever God has placed them for "such a time as this." The most important call on our lives, I believe, is this: to love the Lord God with all our hearts, souls, minds, and hearts. Out of His great love, He called us to be His own. It is a reasonable calling to love Him back.

PRAYERFUL RESPONSE:

As you read through this short list of callings by God, did His Spirit convict you of neglecting one or more of them? Record your thoughts and plans concerning this calling. Take it to your Father in prayer.

_____

_____

_____

_____

_____

_____

_____

_____

CELEBRATE

TODAY'S SCRIPTURE REFERENCE:

*In all this you greatly rejoice, though now for a little while
you may have had to suffer grief in all kinds of trials.*
1 Peter 1:6 NIV

Whenever I travel to California, I am blessed in so many ways. Of course, being with my son, Nick, and his precious family is why I go; being with them is the primary blessing. But it also seems that after every visit, I return home with a spiritual lesson taught to me by my grandchildren. My youngest grandchild, Baxley, has recently taken on the role of a "teacher" and is filled with daily excitement and curiosity. He wakes up knowing that promise and adventure await.

During my last visit, Liam and Bax were already up one morning, eating cereal and playing video games while waiting for everyone else to get up. After getting my morning hugs, I told them my plans to have my coffee, do my Bible study, and then go for a walk. Hoping Baxley would join me as usual, I asked about his plans for the day. Without batting an eye, he very matter-of-factly said, "My plan for today is to play!" *That's a great idea*, I thought!

As we practice living in the light of eternity, perhaps we should adopt Baxley's plan to "play." In other words, practicing the discipline of celebration. Jesus is worth celebrating no matter what we go through—is He not? We live in the In-Between Time, knowing that God can, will, and is making everything new. For this reason, we can celebrate!

God did not just do something special with His creation; He became His creation as the ultimate display of His love. The first Grand Celebration occurred when Love, Joy, and Light pierced the darkness, and an angel proclaimed the birth of the Savior to shepherds. The sky lit up in celebration! We now have a living Hope with an incorruptible inheritance kept in heaven for us (1 Peter 1:3-4). In this, we rejoice even in our trials (1 Peter 1:5). Knowing our Resurrected King's suffering and imminent return empowers us to overcome trials.

Our certainty in Christ allows us to participate in His life and celebrate our inheritance (1 Peter 1:18-19). We can celebrate these things in our everyday lives by participating in Christ's life and doing what He did and would. My son, Nick, put it this way in his devotional, *Fully Forming:*

> *Celebration is an engagement*
> *in the eternal purpose of God.*
> *If we will look for it,*
> *we will see His eternal work in this present reality.*

As we see Him working, we join Him in that work! We can celebrate Him by rejoicing in, enjoying His blessings, and joining Him in His mission to show the world His love.

There is MUCH to celebrate! That's why I like Baxley's plan to play. Our days will be better if we plan to play and rejoice in Jesus, His gifts, and blessings, joining Him in sharing the Good News with others.

PRAYERFUL RESPONSE:

List ways you can celebrate the life of Jesus and the eternal blessings
He has given you.

_____

_____

_____

_____

_____

_____

_____

_____

In what ways will you join Him in His mission to bring the world
into His love and fellowship?

_____

_____

_____

_____

_____

_____

_____

_____

CHASING THE WIND

TODAY'S SCRIPTURE REFERENCE:

And the disciples were filled with joy
and with the Holy Spirit.
Acts 13:52 NIV

One morning, I was late starting out for my walk. It was about nine o'clock, mid-80s, and humid. Thankfully, there was a strong breeze. I walked off my regular route, searching for shady roads and chasing after the wind! How good that stiff breeze felt as I turned the corner, and it struck my face, blowing my hair all over the place. I thanked the Lord out loud for His kindness in supplying that cooling gift.

Then it struck me—I need more than a cool breeze; I need the breeze of His Holy Spirit to pour over me, around me, into me, through me! I found myself singing this hymn in my head:

Spirit of the Living God; fall fresh on me! Spirit of the
Living God; fall fresh on me. Melt me; mold me. Fill me;
use me! Spirit of the Living God; fall fresh on me.

DANIEL IVERSON

Another thing I noticed while walking was that in several places, even when I turned the corner, I could feel the breeze on my back. I was hit with the realization that His Spirit has my back; He is all around me, guiding me, teaching me, and convicting me.

I know that the Holy Spirit dwells in me already as a believer in Jesus Christ as the Son of God, my Redeemer and Savior (Acts 2:8).

The Spirit himself testifies with our spirit
that we are God's children.
Romans 8:16 NIV

I also know that the Holy Spirit moves and breathes life and truth into the hearts of believers (John 16:13).

The book of Acts provides multiple examples where the Holy Spirit moved in amazing ways, filling people to enable them to do the will of the Father. In Acts 4:8, filled with the Spirit, Peter spoke to the rulers and elders of the people. In Acts 4, after praying, the Spirit filled the people who prayed, enabling them to speak the Word of the Lord boldly!

But Stephen, full of the Holy Spirit, looked up to heaven and
saw the glory of God,
and Jesus standing at the right hand of God.
Acts 7:55 NIV

In Acts 13:52, we see that as the disciples were filled with the Spirit, they were filled with joy!

In these examples and others, believers met together in prayer, worship, and fasting, earnestly seeking the Spirit's guidance. In Galatians, however, Paul, in writing to believers there, admonished them for neglecting the Spirit. They had traded walking in the Spirit for working in their own flesh. He said to them:

Did you receive the Spirit by works of the law or by hearing with faith? Are you so foolish? Having begun by the Spirit, are you now being perfected by the flesh?
Galatians 3:2-3 ESV

This scripture hit me hard, especially while I was walking and thinking about it. Walking with the breeze was a joy and was fun. Without the breeze, it was harder and hot.

Oh, how many times do we try to do His good works on our own steam when we could experience His power and joy in the going and doing? Paul told the Galatians that God supplies the Spirit to us, and He works miracles in us and through us by faith. God has given us His Spirit who WORKS through us, not by us WORKING the law!

No wonder we burn out and lose our joy in service. Our service is to be in His power and wisdom, not in our ability, need for recognition and affirmation, or in our own personal agendas.

What if, as we walk through this life, we are like those new believers in Acts? What if we chase after the Holy Spirit, seeking His guidance, power, and wisdom like I was chasing after that cool breeze that morning? What if our works come out of our faith in Him rather than placing our faith in our works? I think we would experience more of the fruit of the Spirit—especially His joy in our service.

PRAYERFUL RESPONSE:

Think about an occasion when you were relying on your own "flesh" rather than His Spirit. Why do you think we often begin with the Spirit but then try to sustain it in our own power? How can you do the works of the Spirit that produce fruit of the Spirit?

_____

_____

_____

_____

_____

_____

_____

_____

_____

CHECKLIST

TODAY'S SCRIPTURE REFERENCE:

I will meditate on your precepts
and think about your ways. I will delight in your statutes.
I will not forget your word.
Psalm 119:15-16 CSB

I am a woman who likes lists (ask my boys who remember chore lists)! Lists allow me to determine what needs to be done and then do it. There's satisfaction in checking off each item as it is completed and the feeling of accomplishment it brings.

But today's list isn't like that. This list, covered by grace and gifted through scripture, is a testament to both wisdom and discipline. This is a checklist to follow under the guidance of the Holy Spirit so that we can have the mind of Christ in practice.

1. Study His Word daily. Focus and meditate on it.
2. Know and believe Who God is and Who He says you are.
3. Ask God to show you lies and misbeliefs that need to be replaced with His truth. Ask Him to help you do it.
4. Ask God to help you decrease so He will increase.
5. Focus on the facts of His Word, not your feelings or the situation; turn your feelings into action when possible (obey).

6. Have an accountability or prayer partner. Satan attacks stragglers.
7. Remind yourself of His benefits. Have a thankful heart.
8. Keep praise on your lips. Sing a song; listen to praise music.
9. Walk in obedience to what you read in His Word.
10. Persevere. Stay alert; the enemy of your soul is lurking around, watching for an opportunity to attack!

Discipline is one of the "spiritual disciplines" that Christians practice, not to earn our salvation or even God's approval. No, it is something we do to live out our salvation. There is nothing we can do to make Him love us more. In fact, discipline draws us closer to Him to know and love Him more!

PRAYERFUL RESPONSE:

From today's reading, list the practices you already partake in and the ones you intend to include. Pray, asking the Lord to help you commit your time to Him.

_____

_____

_____

_____

_____

_____

_____

_____

CHEW THE CUD

TODAY'S SCRIPTURE REFERENCE:

Your words were found, and I ate them, and your words became to me a joy and the delight of my heart, for I am called by your name, O LORD, God of hosts.
Jeremiah 15:16 ESV

L et the record show that I am a city girl. For the sake of illustration, however, we'll pretend that I am a country girl and talk about dairy cows and how they eat. I promise there is a spiritual lesson here!

Dairy cows chew their cud almost 8 hours daily, amounting to approximately 30,000 chews daily. Cow experts say, "A contented cow is one who chews her cud," and there is truth to this statement. The saliva produced when cows chew their cud helps them digest food and make more milk. When a cow chews her cud, she regurgitates her food into her mouth, which she re-chews and re-swallows. Cud chewing makes for a happy, healthy animal.

"That's gross," you say! But think about it for a minute. She chews on her food for a while, swallows it, throws it back into her mouth, and chews on it until it becomes a part of her. She chews the cud to digest it and produce muscle, sinew, and fat. Then, she can produce milk. This sounds similar to what the prophet Jeremiah wrote in today's scripture reference.

How different would our lives be if we "chewed the cud" of God's Word? What if we *ate* His words? Can you imagine the results if we meditated on, studied, and applied God's Word to our hearts and lives as much as 30,000 times per day? What would God produce in our hearts and lives if His Words became a part of who we are?

Repeatedly meditating on His Word might bring us closer to experiencing the mind of Christ, which is something to think about. I bet you never wished you could be like a cow. Ha!

2 Timothy 3:16-17 NCSB tells us that "All Scripture is inspired by God and is profitable for teaching, for rebuking, for correcting, for training in righteousness, so that the man of God may be complete, equipped for every good work." The writer of Hebrews warns listeners not to be lazy or act like spiritual babies who still desire the milk of the Word. He tells them to be mature in their faith and pursuit of discernment of good and evil.

How can you do that without "chewing the cud?" We will never be healthy Christians without devouring God's words until they become a part of what we think, say, and do. That does not happen by attending church and Sunday school or reading the Bible daily. You have to "chew" on the Word—think about it, pray over it, memorize it, study it, and seek to apply it to your life.

Cud chewing typically shows that a herd of cattle is healthy and comfortable. And isn't this true of believers? In a healthy church, members are united with the Father, Son, and each other through love. We see in First Timothy how God uses His Word to equip us "for every good work." In my opinion, loving Him and loving one another is exceptionally good work!

One last thought: Insufficient cud chewing in cows can lead to lower milk fat tests, lameness, and other digestive problems like twisted stomachs. All these problems directly affect their dairy output.

Neglecting to feed on the spiritual meat of God's Word and instead living only on spiritual milk can directly affect your spiritual output. It affects your ability to handle the daily stresses of life or even greater challenges that may come your way. No wonder the writer of Hebrews warned his people to study the Word; he must have loved them very much!

PRAYERFUL RESPONSE:

How much "cud-chewing" do you do daily? How does feeding on God's Word affect your relationship with the Lord? How does it affect how you react to people and circumstances in your life?

_____

_____

_____

_____

_____

_____

_____

_____

CHOOSING THE RIGHT PERSPECTIVE

TODAY'S SCRIPTURE REFERENCE:

*Trust in the LORD with all your heart, and do not rely on
your own understanding; in all your ways know him, and he
will make your paths straight.*
Proverbs 3:5-6 CSB

Glenn and I just returned from a road trip that put 5,000
miles on our car! We started out from Lubbock after
seeing our granddaughter graduate from Texas Tech.
From there, we drove to Amarillo, stopping first at Palo Duro
Canyon (which, if you didn't know it was there, you would miss
it)! You must take a specific road that leads you to the canyon.

As we drove down into the canyon, what we saw left us awestruck.
What we had observed from the top became a whole new
experience at the bottom. We drove through the massive stone
structures, and then the road looped back in a U-turn for the return
trip.

It was amazing to see how different the same formations looked when viewed from a different direction. Glenn also noted that rock formations were impacted by their surroundings, much like life.

Walking through life without considering God's perspective, we still enjoy the beauty around us. We also are impacted by our circumstances, relationships, and thinking. But when we choose (i.e., make the U-turn) to observe and live our lives from God's perspective, we see and experience everything with more joy, peace, and confidence in Him.

The sin that seems so normal, inviting, and okay now, with a God-centered perspective, is seen for what it is. We see the circumstances we thought were okay as dishonoring the One who loves us and gave Himself for us. Seeing our circumstances in this light enables us to live holy, God-honoring lives for and to Him. The confusion, sadness, and discomfort of our situations and relationships seen through our "old lens" can be transformed into trust, joy, and contentment when we view them from His perspective.

Knowing God and believing in His love and grace helps us live and walk in His ways. Out of trust, faith, and acceptance of our identity in Christ, we can have the wisdom and insight to live holy lives that bring glory to Him and blessings to us. Psalms 1:1-3 tells us that a person who lives by God's counsel and wisdom will be like a tree planted by a stream, "yielding fruit in its season and its leaf will not wither. In all he does, he prospers."

The wonderful truth is that when we trust in the Lord with all our hearts and do not rely on our own "stinkin' thinkin" and self-centered counsel, God Himself will make our choices upright, holy, wise, and true! (Linda's interpretation of Proverbs 3:5-6.)

Just like there was only one road leading to Palo Duro Canyon, there is but one road for us believers to travel—His. I pray that we will choose His ways daily over the world's, always seeking to listen to The Voice that whispers, "This is the way; walk in it."

PRAYERFUL RESPONSE:

Examine your life, noting your thoughts, beliefs, and actions. Does your life reflect more of a worldly perspective or God's perspective? In what ways?

_____

_____

_____

_____

_____

_____

_____

_____

Pray, asking your Heavenly Father to guide your thoughts, beliefs, and actions to align with His.

COME

TODAY'S SCRIPTURE REFERENCE:

Come to me, all who labor and are heavy laden, and I will
give you rest. Take my yoke upon you, and learn from me, for
I am gentle and lowly in heart,
and you will find rest for your souls.
For my yoke is easy, and my burden is light.
Matthew 11:28-30 ESV

When our grandson, Baxley, was nearly three years old, his favorite word (besides not!) was "Come!" Sometimes, he said it, and sometimes, he simply called your name and gestured it by waving his hand towards himself. But his intent was very clear either way. He wanted you to come with him because he had a plan in mind for the two of you that involved something he thought was incredibly good for both of you!

Did you know that Jesus does that to you, too? Reread today's scripture, but read it with your name in the place of "all." Jesus is calling you to come to Himself, to come after Him, to follow Him as His disciple.

He calls us to come away from the hard work and legalistic burden of trying to save ourselves or trying to "perform" for His approval. In the context of the day, His listeners were oppressed by the burden of the religious rules and regulations imposed by the scribes and Pharisees. He promised them and us that when we come to Him, we will find rest for our souls.

You see, in Jesus, we find grace and forgiveness. Grace also gives peace and rest. When we come to Jesus in faith, believing in His sacrifice for us as our sin-bearer, we no longer are burdened with guilt or legalistic good works to earn our salvation. Indeed, He has paid the debt of sin for us! Now, we are free to do good works simply because we love Him and appreciate all He does for us.

He also says His yoke is easy and His burden light. He shoulders the burdens with us. "ME" is a heavy burden to carry alone! It is full of selfishness, pride, jealousy, and ingratitude. In Jesus, however, we have been given everything we need to overcome ourselves and walk in a relationship with Him as His disciples.

> And he is before all things and in him
> all things hold together.
> Colossians1 17 ESV

> *. . . are the riches of the glory of this mystery, which is Christ*
> *in you, the hope of glory.*
> Colossians 1:27 ESV

Just as Baxley beckoned me to come outside and enjoy his imaginative plans, Jesus invites us with a twinkle in His eyes. He has a plan in mind for you that involves something He knows is great!

PRAYERFUL RESPONSE:

Jesus is calling you to "Come." What is He calling you to come to and away from?

_____

_____

_____

_____

_____

_____

_____

_____

CULTIVATING JOY IN STINKY FERTILIZER

TODAY'S SCRIPTURE REFERENCE:

Just as the Father has loved Me, I have also loved you;
remain in My love. If you keep My commandments, you will
remain in My love; just as I have kept my Father's
commandments and remain in His love. These things I have
spoken to you so that My joy may be in you,
and that your joy may be made full.
John 15:9-11 NASB

An awful smell greeted me as I walked into the yard one morning in the early spring. It smelled like dog poo—a lot of dog poo! However, Glenn reminded me he had had the yard fertilized just the day before! Man, that fertilizer is stinky stuff! But it gets the job done; our grass is beautiful.

Fertilizers, which contain nutrients that promote plant growth, are usually applied through the soil for plant roots to absorb. They can be organic or inorganic. They occur naturally in compounds such as peat or mineral deposits or are manufactured through natural and chemical processes. Unfortunately, fertilizers don't smell so great, particularly after being watered!

So, what does all this have to do with today's scripture about joy? How can stinky stuff produce joy? Believe it or not, the Bible teaches us that life's trials *can* and *do* promote spiritual growth—including joy!

We all experience some sort of "stinky fertilizer" in our lives. Sometimes, it is a natural consequence of our choices or our "stinkin' thinkin'." Still, at other times, it is manufactured from living in an imperfect world filled with imperfect people. We experience disappointment, tragedy, heartache, afflictions, and struggles that rob us of our joy. But we can let those experiences promote the growth of our joy and other spiritual fruit in our lives.

Jesus tells us to abide in Him and His love so that our joy can be filled up to the top (John 15:9-11)! He has given us His Holy Spirit, which produces joy in us as a fruit (Gal. 5:22-23). Philippians 4:4 emphasizes that our joy is always there for us. We can find true joy by turning to Him regardless of our circumstances. According to James 1:2-4, trials and troubles should be seen as opportunities for joy as they help us grow towards perfection.

Consider it all joy, my brothers and sisters, when you encounter various trials, knowing that the testing of your faith produces endurance. And let endurance have its perfect result, so that you may be perfect and complete, lacking in nothing.
James 1;2-4 NASB

Easy to read. Easy to write. But it is not so easy in the middle of a heartache or trial unless you remember these *facts* over your *feelings*:

Fact 1: God is still God. He is Sovereign. Consider Habakkuk 3:17-19 and Isaiah 46:8-11.

Fact 2: Nothing is impossible for God. Refer to Isaiah 44: 1-8, Isaiah 45:2 and Luke 1:36-37.

Fact 3: God loves you and always does what is best for you. Read Ephesians 3:14-21.

Fact 4: He will never leave or forsake you, abandon or leave you comfortless. Contemplate 2 Thessalonians 3:3, Hosea 2:19-20 and Colossians 1:17.

Fact 5: All things work together for good for those who love the Lord and are called to His service. Read Romans 8:28 and James 1:17-18.

Fact 6: Trials produce the character of Christ in you and bring honor and glory to Him. Review 1 Peter 1:6-7, Isaiah 48:10-11, Hebrews 13:20-21 and 2 Corinthians 4:8-18.

Fact 7: God won't let anything happen in your life that you and the Holy Spirit can't handle in a way that pleases Him. Read 2 Corinthians 12:9 and Psalm 50:23.

Fact 8: He will keep your mind in perfect peace when you focus on Him, trusting Him. He is trustworthy. Consider Isaiah 26:3-4.

Joy is not happiness. Joy is a person, Jesus. He is our Source. If we place Him in the center of every situation, we will have joy—facts over feelings. Speak the truth of God's word to your heart when your feet are mired down in the stinky fertilizer; you will not lose your Joy. You will find Him and grow.

PRAYERFUL RESPONSE:

As you meditated on the scriptures beside each fact, which spoke to your heart today? Knowing that feelings are not good or bad, how can you control your feelings with facts? Don't forget that it's important to acknowledge and address feelings of sadness, anger, frustration, or fear. We should handle them in healthy ways, with truth being the best approach.

_____

_____

_____

_____

_____

_____

_____

_____

_____

DANCING LEAVES

TODAY'S SCRIPTURE REFERENCE:

Consider it a great joy, my brothers and sisters, whenever you experience various trials, because you know that the testing of your faith produces endurance.
And let endurance have its full effect, so that you may be mature and complete, lacking nothing.
James 1: 2-4 CSB

I love the fall, walking down the lane, and watching the leaves "dance" as they fall from the trees. They twist and twirl as the breeze catches them and swirls them through the air, some dancing with partners and some alone. Many dance together as though in a kind of beautiful contagion.

But Glenn simply sees leaves on the ground—leaves he must deal with. Leaves he must rake, blow, gather, and take to the burn pile! Because of the extra work they entail, his perspective on the leaves is entirely different from mine.

In today's passage, James is discussing perspective. We are to consider life a joy! Let's face it: life is full of trials and tribulations. Jesus Himself told us, "In the world, you will have tribulation. But take heart; I have overcome the world," John 16:33 ESV.

Paul instructs us to "rejoice in the Lord always." But how do we cultivate a perspective of joy in the middle of trials and tribulations? Maybe we can take a lesson from the leaves.

Have you ever noticed that some leaves continue to "dance" after falling while swirling across the ground? Peter mentions the same concept as James discussed but also describes the beautiful revelation of our salvation and the Hope it brings.

> *Blessed be the God and Father of our Lord Jesus Christ!*
> *According to his great mercy, he has caused us to be born*
> *again to a living hope through the resurrection of Jesus*
> *Christ from the dead, to an inheritance that is imperishable,*
> *undefiled, and unfading, kept in heaven for you, who by*
> *God's power are being guarded through faith for a salvation*
> *ready to be revealed in the last time.*
> *In this you rejoice, though now for a little while, if necessary,*
> *you have been grieved by various trials, so that the tested*
> *genuineness of your faith, more precious than gold that*
> *perishes, though it is tested by fire,*
> *may be found to result in praise and glory and honor at the*
> *revelation of Jesus Christ.*
> 1 Peter 1:3-7 ESV

The first step in having a joyful perspective during trials is staying focused on Jesus, our Hope, and our future. We can "dance" when we fall on the hard ground of a trial of illness, death, job loss, or broken relationship if we keep our eyes on Him.

We keep our perspective when we remember God is re-creating us through the trial to become more like Jesus. What a sweet thought! I do want to be more like Him, don't you? God is good, faithful, and sovereign. His word in James promises that He is making us stronger in our faith and our character. Believing in Him brings us joy.

We can also find precious, sweet moments—the God moments—in every trial, each day. Let us choose to live in those.

- A child slipping their hand in yours
- A beautiful sunrise or sunset shared with someone you love
- A snuggle at bedtime
- A cup of coffee with your Bible open
- An intimate conversation
- A time when someone shows you grace

Let us look for those moments and live in them through our trials. These moments bring us to a place of worship and thankfulness.

We get to choose our perspective, you know. We determine whether to whine or worship, to be joyful or unjoyful, to dance or drag our feet. I think I will dance!

PRAYERFUL RESPONSE:

Are you experiencing a trial or tribulation? Ask the Lord for grace to see the "beauty in the ashes," then list the blessings He shows you in this trial/tribulation.

_____

_____

_____

_____

_____

_____

_____

_____

_____

DEATH TO SELF

TODAY'S SCRIPTURE REFERENCE:

*Therefore, brothers, by the mercies of God, I urge you to
present your bodies as a living sacrifice, holy and pleasing to
God; this is your spiritual worship. Do not be conformed to
this age, but be transformed by the renewing of your mind,
so that you may discern what is the good, pleasing,
and perfect will of God.*
Romans 12:1-2 HCSB

Shoot fire! Every time I think, "*That dragon is wrestled to the
ground,*" somehow, he pulls a sneaky one, trips me up, and
before I know it, has me pinned down crying, "Calf rope"!
Dying to self is not for the fainthearted. It takes the hardest thing
of all for us humans: total surrender. We do have to cry "Calf rope!"
but not to self, to God.

Dying to self means surrendering everything, including our
dreams, possessions, and relationships, just as Abraham did with
his beloved son Isaac. Dying to self is our priestly service. It is a
choice as we bring ourselves to the altar.

This is our life of worship. It is not called a sacrifice for no reason
or because it is easy. We like being first. We like being the center of
our own worlds and minds. Ah, but Jesus has an upside-down

Kingdom! He tells us that the first shall be last, and the last shall be first. He tells us that whoever loses his life for His sake will gain it.

So, we continually, moment by moment, lay down our "selves" on the altar. We renew our minds with the washing of His Word and abiding in Him. His Holy Spirit enables us to focus on Jesus so that we can, with thankful hearts, submit to His will and His ways.

How thankful we are that His mercies are new every morning. Each day dawns with new hope, new energy, new grace, and new opportunities to be a living sacrifice. We wake up with a choice and continue making choices throughout the day to die to ourselves and live to Christ. I pray we all choose a life of worship today.

PRAYERFUL RESPONSE:

What areas in your life do you need to "die to"? Talk to Him about them.

_____

_____

_____

_____

_____

_____

_____

_____

DO YOU STAND?

TODAY'S SCRIPTURE REFERENCE:

Be alert, stand firm in the faith, act like a man, be strong.
1 Corinthians 16:13 HCSB

I used to own a three-legged wooden plant stand. The legs were screwed into the bottom of the wooden top that was shaped like a bucket. After many years of use, the stool became wobbly. The wood had softened, most likely by the water dripping through the wood slats on the top. This caused the threads to become stripped, so the legs could no longer twist securely into the top. The plant stand could no longer stand firmly.

Have you ever considered how many times God has warned and admonished us in His Word to stand? If you look it up. The word stand is recorded over 600 times in the Bible. In the New Testament, the Greek definition lists these different meanings: to place, to set in place, balance; to make firm; to stand immovable; to stand ready and prepared; to be of a steadfast mind; fix, establish, hold up.

Like my plant stand that no longer stands and has since been thrown away, consider that our faith is like a three-legged stool. Because God never puts anything in His Word that He does not expect us to heed, it would be wise of us to examine carefully and apply His warnings for our "stools" to stand!

The first "leg" is **to stand on the promises of God**. A passage in Hebrews warns us not to be like the Israelites who did not enter the Promised Land because of their unbelief. It is expected of us to trust in every promise made by God. We are to stand mature and fully assured in all the will of God (Colossians 4:12). James tells us in the first chapter of his book that a doubter is like the waves of the sea, being tossed back and forth. Fixing our hearts and minds on His promises establishes our faith.

The second "leg" of our stool is **to stand in awe of the One** who created everything, including us. Listen to Paul's hymn of praise:

Oh, the depth of the riches and wisdom and the knowledge
of God! How unsearchable are his judgments and how
inscrutable his ways! For who has known the mind of the
Lord, or who has been his counselor? Or who has given a gift
to him, that he might be repaid? For from him and through
him and to him are all things.
To him be glory forever. Amen.
Romans 11:33-36 ESV

The third "leg" is **to stand alert to the traps, snares, and ploys of our enemy, Satan**. Jesus Himself told us to "be alert at all times, praying that we may have strength." In Ephesians 6, Paul admonishes us to be strong in the Lord and to put on the full armor of God so that we can stand against the tactics of the devil. We are to stand in His truth, righteousness, gospel, faith, and salvation. We are to wield the sword of His Word.

Peter warns us that God resists the proud but gives grace to the humble. He tells us to cast all our cares on Him because He loves us so very much. But then, he too warns us to:

Be sober-minded; be watchful. Your adversary, the devil, is
prowling around like a roaring lion,
seeking someone to devour.
1 Peter 5:8 ESV

Do you know why he tells you to humble yourself before he tells you to stand? You cannot stand on your own strength. The humble know this. They totally depend on their Father and His strength to stand. 1 Peter 5:10 ESV tells us that Jesus will personally "restore, confirm, strengthen, and establish you." Hallelujah!

Let's go back to the definition of stand. How is your stool standing? Is your faith fixed, established, and firmly placed in the finished work of Jesus Christ? Are you standing immovable on all the promises of God? Is your mind steadfast on the word of God, growing in knowledge and wisdom of the Lord, in awe of Him? Are you alert and prepared for attacks from your enemy? Is your life in balance?

What your stool looks like is not important. It most likely needs a little paint or has a few nicks in it. What is important is that it stands and is useful. I hope you stand and use your gifts well in the work of His kingdom.

PRAYERFUL RESPONSE:

Which leg of your "stool" is a little wobbly? Are you standing on His promises, standing in awe of Him, or standing alert and ready? Pray, asking our Father for a humble heart. One that looks to Him for discernment, strength, a steadfast mind, and dependence on Him through all things.

_____

_____

_____

_____

_____

_____

_____

_____

DON'T BE A BRAT

TODAY'S SCRIPTURE REFERENCE:

For God was pleased to have all his fullness dwell in him, and through him to reconcile to himself all things, whether things on earth or things in heaven, by making peace through his blood, shed on the cross.

Colossians 1:19-20

Has God ever brought you to the place where He has shown you that you are being a brat? It is not a very pleasant place to be in, is it? It is difficult to look into the mirror of your own selfishness and admit to Him and to yourself that you have let the sin of pride control your thoughts and behaviors.

As I looked into that mirror recently, what I saw devastated me. That is not who I want to be, and I know it is not who He wants me to be—a brat! The dictionary defines "brat" as a badly behaved child that is difficult to manage. As a teacher, parent, and school counselor, I have discovered that brats are usually unhappy children. From my experience as one of God's brats, we are generally unhappy, too.

All brats have a few characteristics in common. First, they are **ungrateful**. They want more than necessary, feeling entitled and deserving without gratitude for what they have. For God's children, an ungrateful heart leads down a road of self-centeredness and brings about a loss of the wonder of God and His salvation.

Second, brats **don't listen**. Because of their ungrateful hearts and prideful attitudes, they think they know what's best for them. This, of course, leads to disobedience. Obedience is based on love and trust. Once a brat has crossed the line from gratefulness and humility to ungratefulness and disobedience, love and trust are forgotten.

Missteps down the road of disobedience follow. Often, it is a slow, winding road away from the loving, trusting relationship once held. Other times, it is a steep and immediate incline. But the results are the same: an unhappy "child" needing reconciliation with a loving Father.

Here's the deal, Lucille. In Jesus, all our sins are forgiven, past and present. He forgives our future sins as well because of His grace, mercy, and the Blood that covers us (Colossians 1:19-22). But we muddle up our relationship with Him by being brats. When we come humbly to our Abba (Father) to repent of our selfishness and declare our need for His guidance, our relationship is restored. Declare this to the Lord, "Help me. Quicken my spirit every time I act that way again. I love You, and I desire to love You with my whole heart and actions."

James tells us that when we confess our sins to Him, He faithfully loves, forgives, and restores our relationship. He restores the joy of our salvation and gives us a willing spirit (Psalm 51:12).

How can we have ungrateful hearts knowing what a good God and Father we have? May we never forget. Let's pray for one another. Let us be vigilant to stay in His Word and in His presence. May he provide safe places and build hedges about us to protect us from becoming brats again. The key is we keep thankful and humble hearts, listening ears, and feet that stay on His path of obedience because we keep our hands in His. Then He does the rest.

PRAYERFUL RESPONSE:

Write about a time when you were a brat. Ask His Spirit to show you the underlying sin behind your behavior, whether it was ungratefulness, ignoring Him, or willful disobedience, and ask Him for His help.

_____

_____

_____

_____

_____

_____

_____

_____

_____

DON'T DO THE SPLITS

TODAY'S SCRIPTURE REFERENCE:

*In the bringing many sons to glory, it was fitting that God,
for whom and through whom everything exists,
should make the pioneer of their salvation
perfect through suffering.*
Hebrews 2:10 NIV

U sually, I help Glenn dock the boats by standing or kneeling at the front to guide the boat into the slip. It's my job to grab the sides of the dock to help him steer the boat in without banging into them. More than one time, I've had to step out of the boat to accomplish this, with one foot on the boat and one on the dock. Unfortunately, this has been problematic because you can end up doing the splits if the boat moves away from the dock.

Now, there are several choices when this happens. You can jump onto the dock or quickly jump back to the boat before it moves too far away. Of course, trying to do either of these options is nearly impossible when you are doing the splits. I have yet to fall in the water, but many times, I've used a third option: allow someone on the dock to help me by grabbing their hand and allowing them to pull me onto the dock with a jump.

Lately, I've found myself doing "spiritual splits." On one hand, I have my foot firmly planted on the "dock," God's revelation to me through His Word. This is the Rock of Ages, the loving, gracious, forgiving, just, and holy God. At the same time, I seem to put my foot on the boat of "misbeliefs." Sometimes, my situation or feelings about circumstances cause me to mistrust Him and how He operates in the world. Having my foot on the "boat" affects how I respond to Him and to my circumstances. Much like the boat, the world and its fears and doubts pull me away from God, my dock. This creates the "spiritual splits."

It is funny how we want both sometimes. We want to rest in all the spiritual blessings He promises us as we commit our love and allegiance to Him. Yet, we still want to control "things." Doing the "spiritual splits" can cause us to relinquish our joy, peace, and contentment. James tells us that a doubter is like "the surging sea, driven and tossed by the wind" (James 1:6 HCSB).

So, what shall we do? We grab the hand of our loving Father that is stretched out to us, and we allow Him to pull us back to Himself until our feet are set firmly on the Dock of His promises. Then we stand and keep our eyes on Jesus, the author and perfector of our faith.

Let's remember this precious promise for those of us who sometimes do the "splits."

No temptation has overtaken you except what is common to man. And God is faithful; he will not let you be tempted beyond what you can bear.
But when you are tempted, he will also provide a way out so that you can endure it.
1Corinthians 10:13 NIV

I hope you reach out to the Lord, grabbing His hand to pull you back onto the dock of His love for you when you feel yourself about to fall into the waters of self-reliance. I hope you stand on who He is, believing who you are in Him. Doing the splits can be very uncomfortable.

PRAYERFUL RESPONSE:

In what areas do you have one foot "in the boat of misbelief"?

_____

_____

_____

_____

_____

_____

_____

_____

_____

DON'T FENCE ME IN

TODAY'S SCRIPTURE REFERENCE:

If you hold to My teaching, you are really my disciples. Then
you shall know the truth, and the truth shall set you free . . .
so if the Son sets you free, you will be free indeed.
John 8:31-32; 36 NIV

Our home in Copperas Cove, Texas, was on a small mountain, with our backyard connecting to its side. We had spectacular views and visitors. There were always deer wandering in and out of the brush, coming up the mountain into our yard. Oh, how they loved to eat my flowers. Geraniums were their favorite.

The previous owners had put up a small fence around part of the backyard for their puppy. One afternoon, when I got home from school, there was a fawn caught inside that fence. His mother was standing outside the fence watching him. He would keep running into the fence, trying to get to her.

He couldn't jump the fence because he was too small, and he couldn't find his way back to the gate (which was still open). He would injure himself if he kept running into the fence. So, I gently opened the other gate and maneuvered him back to the open gate. He ran out and back to his mother. They quickly disappeared into the brush and went back down the mountain. I enjoyed watching them run away so freely.

Often, I see myself as that little fawn. Romans 8:2 says that Jesus has set me free from the law of sin and death. Romans 6:18 reminds me I am no longer a slave of sin but of righteousness. At times, I remain confined inside the fence despite the wide-open gate to freedom in Christ. That is what happens when you think you have to live by *works* instead of *grace*. You see, "the Lord is the Spirit, and where the Spirit of the Lord is, there is freedom" (2 Corinthians 3:17 NIV).

Jesus came to preach good news to the poor, proclaim freedom for the prisoners and recovery of sight for the blind. He came to release the oppressed and to proclaim the year of the Lord's favor—His GRACE! (Luke 4:18-19) Salvation is by His Grace. His grace strengthens us and empowers us. Also, grace gives us spiritual eyes to see His truths and to know what grace is! We find freedom through AMAZING GRACE.

Free from what, exactly? Galatians 5 answers this question. Through Christ's grace, we are no longer bound to engage in sinful behaviors such as envy, malice, selfish ambition, impurity, idolatry, hatred, discord, and drunkenness. When we put our faith and trust in Jesus and walk in His grace, we can be free from fear, doubt, worry, and sorrow without hope. We have the freedom to disregard a list of rules that we can't possibly abide by.

But the better side of the coin is what we are free to do. We are free to live by the Spirit. We are free to love one another and to walk in the fruit of the Spirit: love, joy, peace, patience, kindness, goodness, faithfulness, gentleness, and self-control. We are free to experience an intimate relationship with our Heavenly Father, robed in His own righteousness, accepted, loved, and given purpose, identity, and hope for a glorious future with Him.

Wow! I don't think I'll choose the fence; I'm walking out the gate. Do you care to join me? Freedom looks pretty good.

PRAYERFUL RESPONSE:

Have you found yourself inside the "fence" with the gate wide open? What is keeping you from walking out of "the gate"? Talk to the Lord about walking in freedom.

_____

_____

_____

_____

_____

_____

_____

_____

FAMILY

TODAY'S SCRIPTURE REFERENCE:

But when the fullness of time had come, God sent His Son,
born of woman, born under the law, so that He might
redeem those who were under the law,
that we might receive the adoption as sons and daughters.
And because you are sons,
God has sent forth the Spirit of His Son into our hearts,
crying, "Abba! Father!" Therefore, you are no longer a slave,
but a son; and if a son, then an heir through God.

Galatians 4:4-7 NASB

I love my family. I think we are fairly normal, although we have a few oddballs. But they are *our* oddballs. We've had our fair share of extreme highs and lows, times of much love and laughter, and times of sadness and tears. Our family has experienced hurt feelings, jealousy, and angry moments to work through.

But through it all, we are family, united in love and loyalty. We share a bond that strongly supports us individually and corporately. We are The Ackers. If you attack one of us, you face all of us because we stand together as one.

God established the concept of family in Genesis. He created this pattern through which He would set up His Kingdom. His plan through all eternity is to have one people—one family. In Jesus, all are invited to become sons and daughters of God.

We are the adopted children of God; we are His family. This is a sacred, holy Thing. He has set us apart as His chosen people.

> *. . . a royal priesthood, a holy nation, a people belonging for*
> *his own possession, that you may proclaim the excellencies*
> *of him who called you out of darkness into*
> *his marvelous light.*
> 1 Peter 2:9 NIV

Let's think about what is involved in being a part of God's family:

1. His Family loves each other. In John's gospel, Jesus repeatedly says that the world will know about Him because of the love we show to each other.
2. His Family sacrifices for each other. In Philippians 2, Paul encourages us to follow Jesus' example of self-sacrificing love. We are told to not only look after our own interests but also the interests of others.
3. His Family encourages and supports one another. Building up the Body of Christ is essential for the growth of each member. Sometimes, it may involve accountability and truth-telling, which isn't always easy to give or receive.
4. His Family makes memories together, both good and sad. They laugh and cry together. In their journey through life, they grow together in the disciplines of worship, study, meditation, celebration, prayer, and, yes, even fasting.

5. His Family members aggravate each other. Yep, I said it out loud. We do because we are human. We are works in progress, but the good news is that we are of One Spirit, His. Remember, in Galatians, He said that He has placed the Spirit of His Son into our hearts!

His Family stands together as One with Him. That is how we survive as a family. In 2 Thessalonians, Paul encouraged the church to stand firm and hold fast to the Gospel of Jesus Christ, who loved us and gave us eternal encouragement and good hope by His grace. We encourage each other with these truths.

We have only one enemy—the evil one, and we must stand against him and his lies. We do that by following Romans 12, which says, "Let love be genuine. Abhor what is evil; hold fast to what is good. Love one another with brotherly affection. Outdo one another in showing honor and be diligent. Also, be fervent in spirit and serve the Lord. Rejoice in hope, be patient in tribulation, be constant in prayer . . . Live in harmony with one another."

We are the Family of God. When Satan attacks one of us, he faces all of us, including our Father, who has us firmly in His Arms and has equipped us with His own armor (Ephesians 6). What a great family, oddballs and all.

PRAYERFUL RESPONSE:

How does your church family love, encourage, and support you?

_____

_____

_____

_____

_____

_____

_____

In what ways can/do you love, encourage, and support your church family?

_____

_____

_____

_____

_____

_____

_____

_____

FAMILY OF GOD

TODAY'S SCRIPTURE REFERENCE:

*In Christ, we who are many form one body, and each
member belongs to all the others.*

Romans 12:5

That word—family. It conjures up many different feelings, images, thoughts, conceptions, and misconceptions: love, loyalty, laughter and tears, rivalry and jealousy, frustration and anger, fear and respect. Families misunderstand, miscommunicate, misuse, and abuse one another.

But, for the most part, families fiercely love one another and stand by one another through thick and thin. They encourage each other, especially when one of them is under attack. It's like there is some unwritten code: I can pick on my brother, but you had better not!

God, in His ultimate wisdom and sovereignty, put His body together in family units called churches. Each church then bonded together as the Body of Christ. As the body of Christ, we have become:

*God's household, which is the church of the living God, the
pillar and foundation of the truth.*

1 Timothy 3:15

As such, we are to conduct ourselves in ways that exemplify the mystery of Christ and bring glory to His name. You and I know that we are flawed family members, but God does not let us off the hook or change His plan. He simply says to live in peace with one another, to be kind to each other, to rejoice always, and to pray without ceasing. He tells us to avoid every kind of evil and to give thanks in all circumstances. He exhorts us to warn the idle, to be patient with everyone, and to encourage the weak (1 Thessalonians 5:12-16).

In 1 Timothy 3:15-16, Paul tells us that the mystery of godliness is great because it is found in Jesus and in the power of His resurrection. Of course, living as flawed family members in a fallen world, we cannot live the godly lives He has called us to without this power. Imagine the power that it takes to raise someone from the dead.

> *. . . by the power that enables Him to bring everything under*
> *His control, will transform our lowly bodies so that they will*
> *be like His glorious body.*
> Philippians 3:21

Christ is our hope of glory, but He is also our hope of the NOW. God will strengthen us with all power according to His glorious might so that we can have great endurance and patience (Colossians1:11)! The gospel and His truths come to us in the power of the Holy Spirit (1 Thessalonians 1:5). He has given us a spirit of power, love, and self-discipline (2 Timothy1:7).

God's divine power has given us everything we need for life and godliness through our knowledge of Him, who called us by His own glory and goodness. Through these, He has given us His very great and precious promises so that through them, you may participate in the divine nature and escape the corruptions in the world caused by evil desires (2 Peter 1:3-4).

How do we tap into this power? You don't. His Spirit is already there inside you if you belong to Jesus. Yield to Him. Rest in Him. Pray these scriptures over yourself and those you love, asking Him to strengthen you in His power, love, godliness, and self-discipline. This is a prayer He will answer with a resounding, "Yes!" He will sanctify you, grow you, love you, and grace you on this lifelong journey of growing up in God's Household of Faith.

PRAYERFUL RESPONSE:

What kind of "family member" are you in God's household of faith?

_____

_____

_____

_____

_____

_____

_____

_____

_____

How can you become a more loving, gracious, forgiving, and helpful family member? (*Hint: Pray first!*)

_____

_____

_____

_____

_____

_____

_____

_____

_____

FASTING

TODAY'S SCRIPTURE REFERENCE:

Whenever you fast, don't be sad-faced like the hypocrites;
For they make their faces unattractive
so their fasting is obvious to people.
I assure you: They've got their reward.
Matthew 6:16 ESV

Fasting has always been kind of a mystery to me. I mean, you don't eat, right? By nature, I am not one who fasts. But I am learning. We are using our son, Nick's, year-long devotional, *Fully Forming,* to learn and train ourselves in the twelve spiritual disciplines. These include prayer, meditation, submission, fasting, worship, solitude, confession, service, simplicity, study, guidance, and celebration.

I have practiced and enjoyed many of the disciplines for years, but not fasting. Apathy and ignorance are two reasons among many. But Jesus was not apathetic about it at all. He expected, even assumed, that we would fast.

The purpose of all the spiritual disciplines is for training. Each one, when practiced with a heart after God, enables us to "connect with God as He does His gracious work in our lives. They help to move us beyond a fire-insurance faith to develop a personal, intimate relationship with Him on a daily basis." (Nick Acker)

Fasting is an important discipline. It helps us learn to rest in God and in His love and provision.

Nick has led us through two fasts this month. It is a work in progress for me. I must admit the first one was easy; we just had to skip lunch. I learned from that first fast that an important aspect is motive. Jesus, our example, fasted to glorify God, meet with God, and hear from God, not seek to sway God's will to something else. Fasting is submission. I did well on the not eating part; I need to work on the submission part!

The second fast was from lunch to lunch. Spiritually speaking, I gained more insight from this one. Confession time: I dreaded having to give up my morning coffee. As I reached for the coffee cup that was not there, I was so thankful for all the "creature comforts" God gave me that I take for granted every day.

His grace and mercy, His Goodness and love overwhelmed me. I thanked Him for realizing that He provides not only my necessities but also unnecessary blessings, like:

- ✓ beautiful sunsets and sunrises,
- ✓ a warm bed to sleep in, and yes, even
- ✓ flavored coffee with my quiet time each morning.

Fasting has several benefits, which must be why Jesus assumed we would do it. It has a way of aligning and molding our hearts with His. Fasting trains us to focus on Him rather than our appetites; it teaches us to be thankful for His blessings. As we learn to shift our focus onto Him, our eyes and ears are open to hear from Him. The more we hear from Him, the more we trust, love, and rest in Him.

Anna served God by praying and fasting in the temple (Luke 2:36-38). Fasting serves as both a discipline and a service to Him and others. By doing so, we can offer Him a sacrifice of self, submitting our hearts and wills to Him, a living sacrifice of praise!

Like all disciplines, fasting can be dangerous. Jesus wants us to depend on Him, not perform for Him. The disciplines are not about doing something. They are about being with someone. Fasting is not a thing we add to our to-do list of "Things to Do for God." Fasting is Spirit-led, and our motivation is simply to seek His Presence.

As with everything else in being His disciple, I am a learner, a slow one at best. Though it is still somewhat of a mystery to me, I will continue to try to practice this discipline of fasting, one step at a time. I don't think that's too much for Him to ask, considering all He's done for me.

PRAYERFUL RESPONSE:

Have you had a fasting experience? Write about it. Prayerfully consider fasting as a unique way to seek Him.

_____

_____

_____

_____

_____

_____

_____

_____

FINDING PIRATES TREASURE

TODAY'S SCRIPTURE REFERENCE:

All the treasures of wisdom and
knowledge are hidden in him.
Colossians 2:3 HCSB

My sister, Becky, my husband, and I have been holding "Cousins' Camp" for our grandchildren for several years. Each year, we choose a different theme with a scripture to go with it. The theme for 2022 was "It's a Pirate's Life for Me."

We went all out with cannonball fights (water balloons), Grandpa's obstacle course avoiding sharks and walking the plank, swinging over the lagoon, and even a little swordplay. But what would a pirate be without a treasure to seek?

Every year, we hold a treasure hunt. It's a cousin camp tradition. But this year, we made it harder and included a twist at the end with four extra treasure maps. These maps took the cousins on a journey off the property and down the road.

They persevered in the August heat, working together to figure out the clues that led to the maps. They walked many steps to find all the maps that finally led them to the place to dig for their treasure. Oh yes! They had to use a shovel and dig for their treasure, which was $10 bills in burlap bags.

The scripture for the treasure hunt was:

Instruct them to do good, to be rich in good works, to be generous and ready to share, storing up for themselves the treasure of a good foundation for the future, so that they may take hold of that which is truly life.
1 Timothy 6:18-19 NAS

Earlier in the day, we had talked about the fact that Jesus is our treasure. Not only that, but He has also placed His treasure within us, His Spirit, that enables us to be rich in good works, generous, and willing to share. This treasure within allows us to store up treasure in heaven where moth and rust do not destroy. (Matthew 6:20 ESV)

My observation of this for us as believers is two-fold. First, are we seeking His Kingdom, our treasure? Second, how are we helping one another to do this as a community?

The kids worked together as a team to find their treasure. They were of "one mind" as they solved the clues. Furthermore, they supported and motivated each other to press on, even in the heat and fatigue. Despite the difficulty, they remained committed to their task and persevered together.

So, Christian community, I pose the following questions:

- ✓ Do you really believe that all the treasures of wisdom and knowledge are hidden in Christ?
- ✓ How can you live in such a way that you help one another discover all these treasures?

✓ How can you be of "one mind"?
✓ How do you share the wisdom and knowledge He gives you through His Spirit and His Word?
✓ How do you encourage one another to do good works, to be generous, and to be willing to share?

Maybe we all could be a little like the pirates at my house that week—committed to the task and each other and willing to sweat a little to get their treasure. ARRRRR!

PRAYERFUL RESPONSE:

How do you prioritize seeking God's treasures within your church community?

_____

_____

_____

_____

_____

_____

_____

_____

_____

How do you pursue His "treasure" personally?

_____

_____

_____

_____

_____

_____

_____

_____

_____

THE FLASHLIGHT

TODAY'S SCRIPTURE REFERENCE:

*Then God said, "I give you every seed-bearing plant on the
face of the whole earth and every tree that has fruit with
seed in it." God saw all that he had made,
and it was very good.*
Genesis 1: 29-31 NIV

One week, I was in California visiting with my son, Nick, and his family. He and Beka have three children: Zoe, Liam, and Baxley. We had such wonderful times together, playing at the beach and taking walks together in their neighborhood. Living with a two-year-old, Baxley, for a week is a fountain of material for writing a "blog" on spiritual insights! Let me give you just one example.

One evening, Nick was doing something with his flashlight, and Baxley decided he wanted his daddy's flashlight.

"No, Baxley. This is Daddy's flashlight," said Nick.

Then it happened. That pretty face screwed up into a red torrent of tears, and out of that sweet, cherub mouth came, "Daddy, I want that flashlight! You are so annoying!"

"Uh oh," said his daddy. "Looks like you need to go to your room for a reset. Do you want to walk by yourself, or do I need to take you?"

Well, since Daddy was still so annoying, Baxley was taken to his room!

Being an interfering Granna (Do not roll your eyes at me), I waited a few minutes, then went into his room. I pointed out to Baxley all the things that were his to play with—his blocks, books, toy cars. I tried to explain that even though he couldn't play with Daddy's flashlight, he had his own toys to play with. That line of reasoning did not work. Like Daddy, I was annoying!

When I came out of his room, Nick looked at me over the top of his glasses and asked, "So, Mom, how did it go trying to reason with a two-year-old?" (Now you can roll your eyes!)

So where is the lesson? Doesn't this remind you of the oldest story in the Bible? God placed Adam and Eve in the most beautiful place on earth. He gave them all they could ever want or need, including sweet fellowship with Himself. He told them there was only one thing out of all the other things they could have that they could not have—the fruit of the Tree of the Knowledge of Good and Evil.

So, did they say, "Thank you, Father," then and enjoy all the good gifts? Nope. They wanted what they could not have at any sacrifice, even the loss of fellowship with the One who loved them most.

Many believe pride and the desire for self-control and sovereignty are the root of all sin. But ingratitude is, too. How often are we dissatisfied with the gifts God has given us and want more or different? How often do we compare our lives with others and want what they have?

Baxley has a room full of toys. Toys that are much more appropriate for his age level and safety. His daddy loves him and gives him good things. His daddy is also careful to train and discipline him to learn to respect authority and other people, their feelings, and their possessions, just like our Abba, Father. Let us take our lessons to heart (and pray Baxley does, too!).

PRAYERFUL RESPONSE:

Which attributes that only belong to God do you yearn for, like sovereignty, control, knowledge, and worship? Are you dissatisfied with the gifts you have? Pray and ask the Lord for a thankful, trusting heart.

_____

_____

_____

_____

_____

_____

_____

_____

FRAGRANT AROMA

TODAY'S SCRIPTURE REFERENCE:

*But thanks be to God, who in Christ always leads us in
triumphal procession and through us spreads the fragrance
of the knowledge of him everywhere. For we are the aroma of
Christ to God among those who are
being saved and among those who are perishing.*
2 Corinthians 2:14-15 ESV

I love walking down my road, especially in the spring. New flowers are blooming and popping up in the neighbors' yards and the surrounding woods. I first noticed a particular bush not by its appearance but by its smell. I caught the sweetest smell while passing by, which made me stop and search for its source. The bush itself is straggly looking, wild, and crazy. Its branches cascaded down in every direction. But, oh, the fragrance! The fragrance caught my attention before the bush, which got me thinking.

In 2 Corinthians, Paul tells us we are the "aroma of Christ among those who are being saved and those who are perishing." In chapter 2, verse 14, Paul says that God leads us in triumphal procession in Christ and spreads the fragrance of the knowledge of Him through us. The Corinthians would have understood this analogy because the Romans had parades for their returning conquerors. Leading the procession would be slaves waving incense burners. These sweet fragrances were announcing the coming of the conquering heroes.

So, in Christ's triumphal procession, we are the fragrance leading the way. We are spreading the sweet knowledge of Jesus, our conquering hero, and His gospel to those around us. We can do this because His Spirit is in us, enabling and empowering us to walk in the Spirit that produces fruit in our lives. This fruit includes "love, joy, peace, patience, kindness, goodness, faithfulness, gentleness, self-control," according to Galatians 5:22-23 ESV.

Christ Himself is our example of being a sweet aroma. According to Ephesians 5:2, He gave Himself up as a fragrant offering and sacrifice to God. As followers of Jesus, we are to give ourselves daily as fragrant offerings in how we interact with others and share the gospel.

So, back to my thinking. It was not the bush that caught my attention. It was the fragrance. That is how it should be with us. We should be so full of Jesus and devoid of ourselves that we go unnoticed by others. They catch the aroma of Jesus.

PRAYERFUL RESPONSE:

How is your life like a fragrant aroma to the Lord? Are there some areas you need to be sweeter?

_____

_____

_____

_____

_____

_____

_____

_____

_____

A FRIEND LIKE NO OTHER

TODAY'S SCRIPTURE REFERENCE:

No one has greater love than this:
to lay down his life for his friends.
John 15:13 CSB

After years, I finally visited dear friends in Joshua, Texas. These are the kind of friends who just seem to pick up where you left off, no matter how long it's been since you were last together!

We shared old times and new times; we laughed a lot! You could tell that we clearly love each other and have missed our time together. One special thing I noticed was that in the middle of us was another Friend. Almost every one of our conversations would eventually include Jesus.

In our time away from one another, each of us has faced difficult experiences. Some have lost loved ones, some are facing scary illnesses, some are dealing with family tragedies, and all of us have had our faith challenged in some way. Yet, each one attested to the truth that Jesus is our only Hope...that His Redemptive Power both to save, to heal, and to resurrect the dead in His Future Glory is what we cling to.

This brings to mind the precious hymn, "*What a Friend We Have in Jesus,*" by Joseph M. Scriven. Jesus bears all our sins and griefs, our pains and sorrows. He is our faithful Friend who knows our every weakness, Who takes us in His arms and loves and shields us.

The song also reminds us that when we forget to turn to Him in our times of trouble and try to bear our burdens alone, we forfeit our peace and bear needless pain! He is our precious Savior, our Refuge where we can find solace and comfort. As the song says, "Take everything to the Lord in prayer" in our trials and temptations!

It is good to have Christian sisters to turn to for encouragement, comfort, wisdom, counsel, and just plain fun! But it is BEST to have a Friend Who is "closer than a brother," Who loves you like no other and is right there beside you, not minutes or hours away.

Jesus Himself calls us His friends in John 15:13-15 ESV: "Greater love has no one than this, that someone lay down his life for his friends. You are my friends if you do what I command you. No longer do I call you servants, for the servant does not know what his master is doing; but I have called you friends, for all that I have heard from My Father I have made known to you."

Think of it: The Son of the Most High God calls you His friend. A friend is one with whom you have mutual affection and connection. Moreover, a friend is your confidant and companion, someone you trust and have an intimate relationship with. A good friend sticks with you even when you mess up, forgives you, and encourages you along the way!

Can you think of a better friend than Jesus?

PRAYERFUL RESPONSE:

List the ways Jesus has been a friend to you in the past.

_____

_____

_____

_____

_____

_____

_____

_____

_____

FUN & GAMES

TODAY'S SCRIPTURE REFERENCE:

*And whatever you do, in word or deed, do everything in the
name of the Lord Jesus, giving thanks to God the Father
through Him.*

Colossians 3:12-17

To kick off our annual "Summer Nights" meetings for the women of our church, many of us gathered in the Commons Area to play Bunco. Bunco has become one of the most attended activities planned for the women of our church. I think it is because it is just plain fun.

Most people enjoy games for several reasons. We play them to be entertained and to be with people we love or like to be around. Games are fun for passing the time, building memories with family and friends, and connecting with people in a relaxed atmosphere.

We have our favorite games, don't we? Some games are more fun than others. In fact, some games may be frustrating for one person and gobs of fun for another. Some people like games that make you think, while others like games that require no thinking at all. Some games require only two players, and some are more fun with many people. Games vary, just like the people who play them.

Our God is so creative. He made such an amazing variety of people and lumped us all together in a beautiful thing called church, the Body of Christ. He tells us to love one another, build each other up, grow together, share the gospel with the world, and be unified with Him and His Son.

Our Creator has instructed us to:

Put on then, as God's chosen ones, holy and beloved, compassionate hearts, kindness, humility, meekness, and patience, bearing with one another and, if one has a complaint against another, forgiving each other; as the Lord has forgiven you, so you also must forgive. And above all these put on love, which binds everything together in perfect harmony. And let the peace of Christ rule in your hearts, to which indeed you were called in ONE BODY. And be thankful. Let the word of Christ dwell in you richly, teaching and admonishing one another in all wisdom, singing psalms and hymns and spiritual songs, with thankfulness in your hearts to God. And whatever you do, in word or deed, do everything in the name of the Lord Jesus, giving thanks to God the Father through Him.
Colossians 3:12-17 ESV

This is His game plan for us. A church together. A life together. It is messy at times but also filled with love, joy, peace, patience, goodness, gentleness, kindness, faithfulness, and self-control because the Holy Spirit unites us. We gather in thanksgiving, praise, and worship. We gather in sorrow and in happiness. We gather to connect with each other and the One who loves us best.

God doesn't "play games" with us. He lays all His cards on the table in His Word. He tells us who He is, who we are in Him, and how our lives should reflect His image. He pours out His blessings of grace, mercy, love, and forgiveness. He will never "cheat" us in this game of life because He desires our best for His glory together.

PRAYERFUL RESPONSE:

Because we are "goobers," as my son Nick likes to say, some of us are just not that easy to love or be connected to. Yet, God calls us to love even those hard people. Who in your church family do you need to love better? How can you begin to do that?

_____

_____

_____

_____

_____

_____

_____

_____

_____

GET DRESSED

TODAY'S SCRIPTURE REFERENCE:

Therefore, as God's chosen people, holy and dearly loved,
clothe yourselves with compassion, kindness, humility,
gentleness and patience . . . whatever you do, whether in
word or deed, do it all in the name of the Lord Jesus, giving
thanks to God the Father through Him.
Colossians 3:12, 17 NIV

Shopping for clothes is something I love. My mother, sister, and I were about the same size. So, when we'd go shopping together, we each found an armload of cute tops and bottoms and headed for the dressing room.

Of course, we all crammed into the same room and tried on everything. It was so much fun! There was much tugging, sharing, head nodding and shaking, and laughing going on. I am sure the poor woman in the next dressing room wondered what all that cackling was about.

The other super fun thing was when one of us would walk away with a real deal. You know—when you get that cute top for nearly nothing. We never spent the full amount on any purchase. If you are like us in that respect, I have a deal for you!

Your Heavenly Father has given you a beautiful wardrobe. The clothes are dazzling. They are very costly, but He gives them to you as a gift of His Grace through His Son's sacrifice on your behalf. Of course, our main gown as the Bride of Christ is His robe of righteousness (Isaiah 61:10).

It is also part of our Armor of God (Ephesians 6:14). But He has also graced us with additional clothes that add to our beauty. When you wear these garments, you look good. You glow with the radiance of the glory of God.

There is a catch, however. You must take off your old clothes and put on the new ones. In the third chapter of Colossians, Paul explains this to us. Because we have believed in Jesus and are His chosen ones, we are to set our minds on the things above, not on the things of earth. Since we walk with Jesus now, we put off our "old clothes" or practices, such as anger, wrath, slander, lust, greed, impure thoughts, and filthy language, and "put on" our new clothes.

Imagine dressing yourself in these lovely clothes each morning: compassion, kindness, humility, gentleness, love, and patience. Now add the tiara of thankfulness. Even Miss America could not compare with your loveliness as you walk out the door.

Now, why would we leave these amazing clothes hanging in our closets? But we do, don't we? They are ours as gifts of the Holy Spirit, and we are free to put them on at any time. It is time for us to believe we are the daughters of the King and dress like who He says we are.

Will we fall and get the clothes dirty sometimes? Of course. But He is always there to help us up, wipe off the grime, and straighten our tiaras. After all, His mercies are new every morning. We can start with a new "outfit" each day, or even each moment, as we confess and repent of our sins.

When you dress in the morning, wear His clothes of compassion, humility, gentleness, love, and patience, along with your makeup. Do not forget your tiara of thankfulness. A thankful heart is a source of great joy and leads you into the very presence of your Father. He will be delighted to spend time with you and see you in the clothes He gave you.

PRAYERFUL RESPONSE:

Which "accessory" do you most desire to put on each morning: compassion, kindness, humility, gentleness, love, patience, or thankfulness? Pray; talk to the Lord about your desire to exhibit the fruit of the Spirit.

_____

_____

_____

_____

_____

_____

_____

_____

GOT A ROCK IN YOUR SOCK

TODAY'S SCRIPTURE REFERENCE:

Let us also lay aside every hindrance ["speck"!] and the sin which so easily ensnares us. Let us run with endurance the race that lies before us, keeping our eyes on Jesus, the pioneer and perfecter of our faith. For the joy lay before him, he endured the cross, despising the shame, and sat down at the right hand of the throne of God.
Hebrews 12:1-2 CSB [Emphasis added]

Sometimes, when I go for a walk, I get a rock between my sock and my skin. My feet are too skinny, and there is always a gap in my sock between the ankle and heel. So, it is common for me to flip a rock into that gap as I am walking down our roads. This is irritating to me in more than one way.

When this happens, I will continue walking for a bit, trying to ignore the irritant. As I walk, it feels like it is growing, becoming sharper and pointier. It moves around, causing all kinds of havoc in my sock. I do not want to stop. Usually, I am timing myself or am on a schedule. But there it is. Soon, it feels like a boulder; I can no longer think about anything else. The walk is no longer enjoyable. Finally, I must stop and dig that huge rock out of my sock with my finger, only to discover that it is just a tiny speck of a thing. Good grief!

Then I had a thought: *How many times have I walked with Jesus, having a rock in my sock?* As we make our way down this road of life, "rocks" get flipped into our socks that can distract us, hurt us, cause us pain, make us angry and fearful, and take away our joy.

Sometimes, we try to keep on walking with these "rocks" still in our socks. Not good. After a while, not only do we lose our joy and peace of mind, but we start to walk with a limp. Our lives no longer reflect our Savior's character.

So, how do we "dig" out the rocks? First, I think we must recognize that they really are "specks," tiny irritants that are a part of living in a fallen world. Yes, they feel like boulders with spikes, but we do not live by feelings. We live by the truth of the Word of God. Our feelings are real, but we can line them up with His truths. We use His Word to dig out the specks.

What truths do we know about God?
- ✓ I can draw near to the throne of God at any time through Jesus to receive Grace and mercy in time of need. (Hebrews 4:16)
- ✓ He is faithful and keeps all His promises (2 Timothy 2:13)
- ✓ He supplies His very own armor for me to stand my ground against my enemy. (Ephesians 6)
- ✓ The Lord is compassionate and gracious, slow to anger and abounding in steadfast love. (Psalm 103:8)
- ✓ He is a God of Hope (Romans 15:13), and Christ in me is my hope of glory. (Colossians 1:27)
- ✓ He sustains all things and holds all things together. (Colossians 1:17) Remember: *that includes you and me!*

✓ He keeps us in perfect peace when our minds are stayed on Him because we trust in Him. He is our everlasting Rock. (Isaiah 26:3-4)

These are just a minute sample of the vast promises and truths that God has given us in His Word to sustain us and to enable us to "dig" out the specks in our socks. Hebrews 12:1-2 assures us we can run with endurance when we fix our eyes on Jesus, the author and perfector of our faith.

Let's keep our socks clear of rocks so we can stay focused on Jesus instead of our feet!

PRAYERFUL RESPONSE:

Write down the scriptures that help you regain your focus on Jesus when faced with obstacles.

_____

_____

_____

_____

_____

_____

_____

_____

Handling feelings in a healthy manner is crucial. How can you acknowledge your feelings and bring them captive to Christ?

_____

_____

_____

_____

_____

_____

_____

_____

_____

GRACE IS BEST

TODAY'S SCRIPTURE REFERENCE:

For you are saved by grace through faith, and this is not from
yourselves; it is God's gift—not from works,
so that no one can boast. For we are His creation,
created in Christ Jesus for good works,
which God prepared ahead of time
so that we should walk in them.
Ephesians 2:8-10 HCSB

For most of my life, I have believed in a "grace plus works" doctrine without even realizing it. I will confess it has been a burden for this performance-oriented woman. Yes, I have believed that God's salvation is His gift of grace, but I have been taught that as a believer, there are certain things that I have to do.

In my desire to please God, I became a slave to those "things to do." Instead of becoming an "end to the means," they became as important as the "Means." I lived under so much spiritual pressure, trying to reconcile grace and my "works." I would feel so guilty when my "doing" got off track. Was God disappointed in me? Was He frustrated with my progress or lack thereof?

Over the last few years, I have come to the realization that grace is best. It is a gift with no strings attached, just wrapped up with a big, beautiful bow of love. Jesus is everything. If that is true, then all the "have to's" are not anything but a means to make a way for me to see that Jesus, indeed, is everything.

The book of Ephesians teaches this:

> *For you are saved by Grace through faith, and this is not from yourselves; it is God's gift—not from works, so that no one can boast. For we are His creation, created in Christ Jesus for good works, which God prepared ahead of time so that we should walk in them.*
>
> Ephesians 2:8-10 HCSB

I've always had the cart before the horse. I've been doing good works towards pleasing God and staying in His good Graces when I've already been there all along. Right now, in my identity in Christ, I have all the love of God, all His forgiveness, all the spiritual blessings in the heavenly places (Ephesians 1:3).

Now, you may say, "But the "doing" is important. What about Bible study, prayer, worship, and service? And what about confessing when we sin?" The answer is "Yes!" Those things are very important because they all train us to walk in a manner pleasing to Him.

Here's the difference: I do those things from a position of resting in His Grace, knowing I can never do, say, or think anything to make Him love me more or less or make me acceptable to Him. I do not have to do good works to be good. Jesus' blood makes me good.

Knowing that I will make mistakes, I still practice those things, and He will show me grace as I confess and grow in Him. With open hands, I come to Him, embracing His grace and forgiveness.

As I practice the disciplines of prayer, study, meditation, worship, service, submission, confession, and celebration, I am training my heart and mind to be in a place to be transformed by Him. The more I practice and receive His grace, mercy, love, forgiveness, wisdom, and guidance, the more motivated I become to practice.

I admit I still rely on "works" often but will keep training. It's more enjoyable to approach His good works from a grace perspective; it alleviates guilt and worries about reconciling works and grace. Grace is best.

PRAYERFUL RESPONSE:

Have you struggled with a "works perspective"? In what way? How can you rest in His Grace?

_____

_____

_____

_____

_____

_____

_____

_____

_____

GRACIOUS, PEOPLE

TODAY'S SCRIPTURE REFERENCE:

*For the grace of God has appeared, bringing salvation for all
people, training us to renounce ungodliness and worldly
passions, and to live self-controlled, upright, and godly lives
in the present age.*
Titus 2:11-12 ESV

My friend Kalina Collier and I just wrapped up our inductive study of Titus. It took us five months to work our way through Paul's instructions to Titus on the island of Crete. We spent many nights laughing, crying, and looking at one another with big eyes of wonder at how the Spirit can reveal one insight to one of us and a completely different one to the other. Studying His Word together, word by word, thought by thought, precept upon precept, is just plain fun. And convicting!

Paul spoke to Titus about teaching sound doctrine to his people. He taught that you cannot have sound faith or sound behaviors without sound doctrine. Further, he gave instructions on how elders, older women, and young men and women should behave. Then, in chapter two, Paul gives instructions about grace.

God's grace, merciful kindness, and totally undeserved favor bring us salvation, turn us to Christ, and train us in Godly living. Indeed, grace allows us to practice Christian virtues of self-control and right living, thus denouncing ungodliness and worldly ways. His grace redeems, reforms, and rewards us with eternal life! (Wiersbe) God's grace is a transforming grace teaching me how to live. It strengthens, encourages, sustains, and empowers me to deny worldly living, live a sensible life of self-restraint, and practice righteous living.

Kalina and I noticed that Paul mentions "good works" six times in these three chapters. By our good works, we put Christ on display! We are to adorn our lives with holiness that draws attention to Him in us. The only way we can do that is through His grace. Grace gives us the desire, zeal, and motivation to do the works He has prepared us to do. God's grace is amazing and unexplainable.

Paul's final instructions were:

> *And let our people learn to devote themselves to good works,*
> *so as to help cases of urgent need,*
> *and not be unfruitful.*
> Titus 3:14 ESV

Kalina and I spent a long time talking about how you learn to practice good works. What does "devoted to good works" look like? How do you teach others to practice good works?

One thing is that we must stop being entitled believers. We must stop behaving as if we deserve God's grace. His grace should once again be a wonder to us. It makes us drop to our knees in awe and thankfulness, humbly whispering, "Why me, Lord?" Then we take His hand, let Him help us stand, and say, "What now, Lord?"

Paul's final word to Titus is, "Grace be with you." It made me consider how we can extend grace to those around us, letting the grace we receive overflow onto them.

Here are some suggestions:

- ✓ Give people the favor God gives you when you do not deserve it.
- ✓ Bless people with words of encouragement...kind in words and tone.
- ✓ Have kind, gracious actions.
- ✓ Pray for them.
- ✓ Spend time with them when it is not convenient for you.
- ✓ Love them with the truth.
- ✓ Listen.
- ✓ Forgive them; show mercy over judgment.
- ✓ Think gracious thoughts about them. Thoughts will affect your actions towards them.

Goodness, people! How can we not be gracious when so much grace has been given to us?

PRAYERFUL RESPONSE:

To whom do you need to show grace? Considering the grace given you by God, what specifically can you do to show grace to them?

_____

_____

_____

_____

_____

_____

_____

_____

_____

GRATITUDE

TODAY'S SCRIPTURE REFERENCE:

*When I heard these things, I sat down and wept. For some
days I mourned and fasted
and prayed before the God of heaven.*

Nehemiah 1:4

BREAK MY HEART FOR WHAT BREAKS HIS

As I walked down my road one morning, I was thinking and praying about everything happening in our world today. I asked the Lord to break our hearts for what breaks His. This led me to wonder, *What breaks the heart of God?*

Is it injustice? Yes. Is it cruelty to another human being? Yes. Is it sexual impurity? Yes. Is it slander and gossip? Yes. It is all these sins, but what is at the core?

Romans 1:21 says, "For although they knew God, they did not honor Him as God or *give thanks to Him*, but they became futile in their thinking, and their foolish hearts were darkened." [Emphasis added]

In his book *Total Forgiveness*, Dr. James Kennedy suggests that "an ungrateful person is only one step away from getting his or her needs met in illegitimate ways." Ingratitude is the initial step that distances us from God and leads us to commit other sins.

Ingratitude is a lack of humility, a choice we make to deny who God is and our relationship with Him. It is one of our enemy's favorite tools to put us out of sorts with God, with our circumstances, and with our relationships. This leads to bitterness, envy, hatred, betrayal, slander, impurity, unforgiveness, etc. We pay an incalculable price for ingratitude.

Let us, then, with humble and happy hearts, choose gratitude. Ellen Vaughn says," Gratitude unleashes the freedom to live content in the moment, rather than being anxious about the future or regretting the past." It takes a grateful, humble heart to cast all your cares on Jesus.

Oswald Chambers says, "The thing that awakens the deepest well of gratitude in a human being is that God has forgiven sin."

Nancy Leigh DeMoss suggests that believers, having been born with inescapable guilt, have received undeserved grace, which should lead us to abounding gratitude. She asks, "Why are we whiners instead of worshippers?"

For one thing, it is not in our nature—not our original sinful nature, that is. Ingratitude is all about us, our needs, our hurts, our feelings, and our desires. Ungrateful people are complainers, always demanding their rights. On the other hand, grateful people seek to bless others and see God as the giver of gifts. They are content and joyful, impacting those around them with a sense of calm and confidence in the goodness of God.

A grateful heart is the fruit of 1000 choices. It is a godly habit that we develop as a lifestyle. Gratitude becomes our spiritual sacrifice of praise. Psalm 22:3 says that God inhabits the praises of His people. Praise and thankfulness are spiritual walking buddies. Praise is the spark plug of our faith.

I don't know about you, but I choose to be a worshipper instead of a whiner. I have specifically asked the Lord to make me sweet. For him to quicken my spirit any time ungratefulness rears its ugly head. And He has. It's uncomfortable because He's had to do it a lot! I am not as grateful a person as I thought I was. I do more than my fair share of whining. But now that I am aware, I have committed to choose gratefulness one choice at a time. He is faithful and just to complete the work that He began in me (Philippians 1:6). Which is one more thing to be thankful for.

If you would like to learn more about living a life of gratitude, I recommend the book *Choosing Gratitude* by Nancy Leigh DeMoss.

PRAYERFUL RESPONSE:

Are you a whiner or a worshipper? How can you train yourself to live with a thankful heart?

_____

_____

_____

_____

_____

_____

_____

_____

THE GREAT EXCHANGE

TODAY'S SCRIPTURE REFERENCES:

*All we like sheep have gone astray; we have turned—every
one—to his own way; and the Lord has laid on him the
iniquity of us all.*
Isaiah 53:6 ESV

*For our sake he made him to be sin who knew no sin, so that
in him we might become the righteousness of God.*
2 Corinthians 5:21 ESV

There is not a woman alive who doesn't understand the beauty of exchange. We have all experienced purchasing something to get it home and discovering it doesn't fit, or "go with," or that it is not even what we really wanted to begin with! So, we returned it to the store and happily exchanged it for what we wanted.

In the human economy, exchanging is the "act of giving one thing and receiving another (usually of the same type or value) in return." It's like a trade or swap. However, an exchange takes on a different persona in God's economy: His.

In the gospel of Mark, Jesus revealed Himself as Israel's long-awaited Redeemer, as prophesied by Isaiah:

*For the Son of Man came not to be served but to serve, and
to give his life as a ransom for many.*
Mark 10:45 ESV

Jesus came to set up the Upside-Down Kingdom, a kingdom where humility, graciousness, servanthood, and love are revered over power, greed, and control. To set up the Kingdom, the Great Exchange occurs between God and His creation, us.

Our natural inclination is toward power, greed, and control, in other words, sin. Left on our own, we will always default to that; there is no hope for our reconciliation with God. We are in desperate need of a Redeemer.

When Jesus died on the cross, God placed on Him the consequences for my sins and yours. God looked at Jesus as though He had committed every sin that had ever or would ever be committed by His people. Then God poured out all His righteous wrath against that sin on Jesus!

The Great Exchange took place at the cross. Jesus took my sin, your sin, and gave us His righteousness in exchange. So now, as a believer in Jesus as my Savior and Lord, when God looks at me, He sees the righteousness of Jesus! Incredible. Unfathomable. The wonder of the cross is not only that God forgives our sins but that He also looks at those of us who are in Jesus as though we have perfectly kept His commands! Oh, what a Savior! Isn't He wonderful?

This is who we are in Jesus: Righteous, Beloved, Accepted, Forgiven, Blessed! This is our identity, our reality. How, then, shall we live from the perspective of The Great Exchange...our sin for His Righteousness? How shall we worship Him and celebrate this amazing life we've been given in His eternal Kingdom that has already begun? How does He love us? Let us count the ways!

PRAYERFUL RESPONSE:

I invite you to pray, asking God to daily remind you of His incredible gift to you. Ask Him to show you ways to live your life that reflect His righteousness and to enable you through His Spirit to do the things He shows you.

_____

_____

_____

_____

_____

_____

_____

_____

_____

HAPPY THOUGHTS

TODAY'S SCRIPTURE REFERENCE:

Finally, brothers and sisters, whatever is true, whatever is honorable, whatever is just, whatever is pure, whatever is lovely, whatever is commendable-if there is any moral excellence and if there is anything praiseworthy—
dwell on these things.
Philippians 4:8 CSB

My grandkids love to go for night walks at the lake. With flashlights in hand, we cautiously walk down the oil-based path, feeling a tad uneasy about the unknown that awaits us. Of course, it doesn't help that a certain grandmother and great-aunt have scared the pants off them in the past.

One night, the three girls, Seth, and I, took off into the darkness with tall, shadowy trees looming on either side of us. As we walked along and talked about what creatures we might encounter, Seth, who was seven, decided to turn back.

But the girls wouldn't have it. Before a "major event" took place between them, Granna intervened and suggested that Seth think happy thoughts to keep himself from being afraid. He wanted to know what that was, so the girls and I suggested some happy thoughts.

"Ice cream," shouted one! "Birthday parties," said another. Seth began to get the idea, so then the "Happy Thought Game" began, and we proceeded down the dark road again. Until Seth got mixed up and yelled out, "MONSTERS!" Then he stopped in his tracks, looked at all of us with big eyes, and said, "That's NOT a happy thought!"

We all busted out laughing, continuing our way. Of course, we didn't get very far until someone's flashlight picked up the gleam of a creature's eyes shining in the woods. That did it. "MONSTER!" Seth screamed. We all ran home, laughing and screaming at the same time.

I tell this story to remind myself and you that Jesus is not only our happy thought but also walking with us down the dark, scary roads in our lives. I know because my family has walked down some roads these past four years that have been very difficult, dark, and scary. The dark road and unknown scenery evoke feelings of fear and doubt in me.

By centering my thoughts on Jesus and His unwavering love for me and remembering His assurance to always be by my side, I can shift my mindset from fear and doubt to peace and gratitude.

Over the years, God's Word has been the best source of happy thoughts. For example, Colossians 1:17 CSB says, "He [Jesus] is before all things, and by him, all things hold together." [Emphasis added.] Interestingly, I've written "He keeps me intact!" beside that verse in my Bible.

What a comforting thought. Jesus sustains me through everything and every situation I experience. The second chapter of Ephesians is a source of happiness that fills me with thankfulness.

> *But God, who is rich in mercy, because of his great love that*
> *He had for us, made us alive with Christ even though we*
> *were dead in trespasses. You are saved by grace!*
> Ephesians 2:4-5 CSB

You get the idea. God's Word, His Truth for us, keeps our hearts and minds focused on things that are true, honorable, just, pure, lovely, and commendable (Philippians 4:8), thus allowing us to experience Christ's peace.

I would suggest that you make a few index cards of verses "happy cards" to keep in your purse, on your mirror, or on the windowsill in the kitchen. There was a dark time when I kept mine in my purse to be read while I waited in line at Wal-Mart or Chick-fil-A.

So, if your mind and heart are filled with fear, anxiousness, and doubt due to "monsters" in your thoughts, whip out your "happy cards" of the Word of God and fill your mind with His Truth, thus renewing your mind to have the mind of Christ.

Now, that is a happy thought!

PRAYERFUL RESPONSE:

Make a list of your favorite "Happy Thoughts." If you like, transfer them to index cards to keep handy when needed.

_____

_____

_____

_____

_____

_____

_____

_____

_____

HARD SAYINGS OF JESUS

TODAY'S SCRIPTURE REFERENCE:

If anyone loves Me, he will follow My word; and My Father
will love him, and We will come to him, and make Our abode
with him. The one who does not love Me does not keep My
words; and the word which you hear is not Mine,
but the Father's who sent Me.

John 14:23-24 NASB

In John 6:51-60 NIV, Jesus is teaching the Jews about His being: "I am the living bread that came down out of heaven; Whoever eats of this bread will live forever. The bread is my flesh, which I will give for the life of the world." The Jews argued with one another, not understanding. Even His disciples, when they heard, said, "This is a hard saying; who can hear it?"

When you read through the Bible following a daily plan, you come across some hard sayings of Jesus that open the door to many questions. In Matthew 16, Jesus and His disciples went to Caesarea Philippi, where He asked them who people were saying He was. They told him that some said He was John the Baptist, others Elijah, Jeremiah, or one of the other prophets. Peter spoke up and said,

"You are the Christ, the Son of the living God." Jesus blessed Peter and told him that God had revealed that truth to him. He told Peter He would build His church upon that faith.

Then, down the road, Jesus tries to prepare them for His upcoming suffering, death on the cross, and resurrection on the third day. But Peter takes Jesus aside and rebukes Him, telling Him that this should never happen to Him. Then Jesus, turning on him, rebuked him, calling him Satan. Jesus told Peter he was a hindrance and stumbling block to Him. His mind was not aligned with God's agenda but his own.

Now, that is a hard saying. Peter, out of his deep love for Jesus, allowed himself to be aligned with Satan's plan to deter Jesus from the purpose for which He came. For this, he was harshly rebuked.

My first thought was one of soul-searching. How have I aligned myself with Satan's plans when I pursued my agenda over the Lord's? How had I been a hindrance and a stumbling block to His plans and purposes?

Here's the part that is so precious about our Jesus, an ever-compassionate teacher. In the very next verses, He explains to them carefully what it means to be His disciple, to follow Him and His agenda. He talks to them about denying self, taking up a cross, and following Him. He talks to them about an upside-down kingdom where you lose your life to save it.

I know it was hard for Peter to hear that rebuke from His Lord. It must have been especially difficult after having just received that blessing. It's hard for us to read this passage knowing that it directly applies to us. But it also makes me so thankful for grace, compassion, forgiveness, and the teaching I can gain from His Word when I open myself to receive it into my heart and mind.

Besides, how can I apply His teaching to my life until I humbly accept it? We must work our way through the hard sayings of Jesus if we are to truly be His followers. That's just how it goes.

PRAYERFUL RESPONSE:

What are some hard sayings of Jesus that you have had difficulty with? Pray and ask your Father to give you understanding and empower you to obey.

_____

_____

_____

_____

_____

_____

_____

_____

HE CARES FOR YOU

Peace I leave with you; my peace I give you, I do not give to you as the world gives. Do not let your hearts be troubled and do not be afraid.

John 14:27 NIV

Today, I will tell you a story and then let the Word of God wash over you. His Word declares that we are righteous by faith, giving us His peace through our Lord Jesus Christ (Romans 5:1)

One very cold day, I was out on my usual walk. Even though it was bitter outside, I continued to walk, bundled up in my warm jacket, hat, and gloves. While looking up, I saw my favorite bluebirds sitting on the high wires. They were so pretty with their bright orange chests and blue backs and wings.

Without a doubt, their songs to one another were cheerful and like music to my ears. I was concerned about them in the cold and curious about how they stayed warm in the chilly breeze. So, I researched the internet.

Did you know that birds stay warm by trapping pockets of air around their bodies? The secret to maintaining these layers of air lies in having clean, dry, and flexible feathers. They accomplish this by a cleaning process called "preening."

Isn't that interesting? But more than that, isn't it just like our God to provide for even a bluebird to stay warm in the cold? Jesus said:

But even the hairs of your head have all been counted.
So don't be afraid;
you are worth more than many sparrows.
Matthew 10:30-31 CSB

Philippians 4:6-7 CSB says this: "Don't worry about anything, but in everything, through prayer and petition with thanksgiving, present your requests to God. And the peace of God, which surpasses all understanding, will guard your hearts and minds in Christ Jesus."

My prayer is to be more like the bluebirds and just naturally do what God has already placed inside me to do: trust Him. He has placed His Spirit in me as I accepted Jesus as my Savior, giving me hope, peace, joy, love, security, forgiveness, provision, protection, mercy, and grace, to name just a few of the spiritual blessings. I hope I sing, don't you?

The LORD is my strength and my song; He has become my
salvation. This is my God, and I will praise Him,
my father's God, and I will exalt Him.
The LORD is a warrior; Yahweh is His name.
Exodus 15:2-3 HCSB

Though the fig tree does not bud, and there is no fruit on the vines, though the olive crop fails and the fields produce no food, though there are no sheep in the pen and no cattle in the stalls, yet I will triumph in Yahweh; I will rejoice in the God of my salvation! Yahweh, my Lord is my strength; He makes my feet like those of a deer and enables me to walk on mountain heights!
Habakkuk 3:17-19 HCSB

But You, LORD, are a shield around me, my glory, and the One who lifts up my head. I cry aloud to the LORD, and He answers me from His holy mountain.
Psalm 3:3-4 HCSB

I keep the Lord in mind always. Because He is at my right hand, I will not be shaken. Therefore my heart is glad, and my spirit rejoices; my body also rests securely.
Psalm 16:8-9 HCSB

PRAYERFUL RESPONSE:

List ways God has provided for you and your family. Meditate on the scriptures given above, thanking God for His provision for you.

_____

_____

_____

_____

_____

_____

_____

_____

_____

HERE COMES A MIRACLE

TODAY'S SCRIPTURE REFERENCE:

When Jesus landed and saw a large crowd, he had compassion on them . . . "How many loaves do you have?" he asked. "Go and see." When they found out, they said, "Five— and two fish." . . . Taking the five loaves and the two fish and looking up to heaven, he gave thanks and broke the loaves. Then, he gave them to his disciples to distribute to the people. He also divided the two fish among them all. They all ate and were satisfied, and the disciples picked up twelve basketfuls of broken pieces of bread and fish.

Mark 6:34-44 NIV

Did you know that the miracle of feeding the five thousand is the only miracle Jesus performed that is recorded in all four of the gospels? I've learned that God repeats Himself because he really wants us to understand what He is saying. So, what is it that He wants us to learn from this particular miracle?

First of all, Jesus allowed Himself to be interrupted from a very special, private time with His disciples to welcome this crowd of five thousand men (back then, women weren't counted in the number). They had followed Him to a place outside the town of

Bethsaida. He taught them and healed some of them out of His compassion for them. Is your heart so filled with compassion for others that you would give up something you are enjoying to help a friend, much less a stranger?

Secondly is the miracle itself. I like to think that some interruptions can lead to miracles. It definitely did in this case. Can't you picture the twinkle in Jesus' eyes when the disciples told him there was no food for all these people, and He told them, "You give them something to eat!"

How quickly they had forgotten that He had calmed the wind and waves and brought a dead girl to life! But what about us? How quickly do we forget in Whom we have put our faith and trust?

I love the part when Jesus personally involved the disciples in the miracle itself. You see, after Jesus looked up to heaven and gave the blessing, He took the five loaves and two fishes, broke them, and "Gave them to the disciples to set before the crowd, and they all ate and were satisfied." (Mark 6:42 ESV)

The multiplication of the loaves and bread occurs in the process of serving them to the people. Can you imagine the wonder in the disciples' hearts as they watched this miracle unfolding within their hands? Wow. Minds blown!

There are two more things to consider here. One, Jesus satisfies. He is more than enough. He fills us up with His love, mercy, and grace, ready to meet our every need.

Secondly, Jesus works miracles. I don't want to miss them, but to actually be a part of them. Don't you?

Consider the miracles we get to see in every ordinary day:

- ✓ the miracle of a sunrise or sunset
- ✓ the miracle of the birth of a baby

- ✓ the miracle of a spiritual rebirth
- ✓ the miracle of our own sanctification
- ✓ the miracle of love between a husband and wife, a mother and child, or a father and child
- ✓ the miracle of healing
- ✓ the miracle of friendships
- ✓ the miracle of spiritual gifts
- ✓ the miracle of provision

I could go on and on. The best is the miracle that "God so loved the world that he gave his only Son that whoever believes in him should not perish but have eternal life" (John 3:16 ESV). And, of course, the miracle that He is coming back!

The disciples were part of the miracle because they obeyed Jesus and did as He instructed. They had the people sit down in an orderly way, and they passed out the food. How exciting that our own obedience can allow us to experience one of Jesus' miracles.

> Here comes a miracle, Here comes a miracle,
> Can't you feel it in the air?
> That look is on His face; His glory is in this place.
> And I know a miracle is near!
> STEVE MILLIKAN/RAY BOLTZ

PRAYERFUL RESPONSE:

What miracle do you need from God? Talk to Him about it. Record your thoughts. What miracles have you already witnessed?

_____

_____

_____

_____

_____

_____

_____

_____

_____

HIS CHILD

TODAY'S SCRIPTURE REFERENCE:

*But to all who did receive Him, He gave them the right
to be children of God, to those who believe in His name,
who were born not of blood, or of the will of the flesh,
or of the will of man, but of God.*
John 1:12-13 HCSB

This scripture is an amazing truth to meditate on. In fact, if you think on it long enough, your heart is filled with awe and gratefulness at the incredible grace and mercy of our Loving Father.

It is by His will that you and I are His kids. We did not wish it, will it, or even want it. He first loved us and called us to Himself, enabling us to believe in His Son and His purpose, giving us the right to be called His children. It was His will first, and then it became mine and yours.

He loved us long before we ever loved Him. He loved us when we were ugly, dead in our sin, full of rebellion, when we were "children of wrath," following our own fleshly desires and snubbing our noses at Him.

But God, who is rich in mercy, because of His great love that
He had for us, made us alive with the Messiah.
Ephesians 2:4-5 HCSB

Now, we walk in His grace. We live and breathe in freedom. We are children of the most high God, and He delights in us.

The LORD delights in those who fear him, who put their
hope in his unfailing love.
Psalm 147:11 NIV

We stand before Him wrapped in the righteousness of Jesus, perfectly pure and fully accepted. We do not have to perform to earn or keep His love. Our Father simply loves, accepts, and delights in us and supports us in our pursuit of Him now.

In Mark 10:13-16, Jesus told the disciples to let the little children come to Him. He used a child as an example of how we are to come to Him. Thoughts of my grandson come to mind. Whether I am at my Baxley's house or mine, he just wants me to be with him and play together.

That is what Jesus means. We are to come to Him eagerly, lovingly, and simply wanting to be with Him. We know He wants to be with us too. What peace would we have if we approached God knowing we have nothing exceptional to offer Him, confessing we cannot navigate life without Him, and listening to and trusting Him like the Father He is?

Surely, we can find time each day to just be with our Abba Father, who paid an incredible price to be with us.

PRAYERFUL RESPONSE:

Take a few minutes to meditate on John 1:12-13. Sit in His Presence, thanking Him for His love for you.

_____

_____

_____

_____

_____

_____

_____

_____

_____

HIS MASTERPIECE

TODAY'S SCRIPTURE REFERENCE:

For we are His workmanship,
created in Christ Jesus for good works,
which God prepared ahead of time for us to do.
Ephesians 2:10 CSB

This scripture is incredible to think about, isn't it? The Creator of the universe formed mankind out of nothing and made us something. Then He took it one step further and did something breathtaking. He regenerated men and women in Jesus into masterpieces.

In the beginning, He breathed life into humanity. In the new birth, He breathes His Holy Spirit into men and women so that they will do the good works He had already prepared for them to do. Wow!

The great teacher and preacher Charles Stanley used an effective illustration regarding this in one of his sermons. There was an art enthusiast who was visiting an art museum specifically to see paintings from one of the old Masters. There was a painting that he was particularly anxious to examine. Imagine his disappointment when he saw that the painting had been removed for cleaning!

The workers sometimes take down the masterpieces to clean them since they get dirty hanging in the gallery day after day. The dirt and grime do not lessen their value or make them less of a masterpiece, but the cleaning helps to maintain their life and beauty.

The same is true for us. Sometimes, our lives get dirty and grimy from the filth of living in this world. The dirt and grime do not change the fact that we are His masterpieces or that we are beautiful in His sight. Yet, the accumulation of dirt and grime suggests a spiritual cleaning is necessary.

2 Corinthians 5:17 tells us that if anyone is in Christ, he is a new creation; the old has gone, the new has come. But we all know that sometimes we sin. We allow the world to get our hands and feet dirty. But we also know that:

> *If we confess our sins, He is faithful and righteous to forgive*
> *us our sins and to cleanse us from all unrighteousness.*
> 1 John 1:9 CSB

The Lord breathes new life into our hearts through confession, repentance, and forgiveness. Our walk with Jesus renews us, bringing joy, peace, and contentment. The good works that He has purposed us for seem to just spring forth from us as He shows them to us. We step into them with obedient, grateful attitudes.

Praise God from whom all blessings flow. Praise Him for His plan of regeneration that makes us His masterpieces. Praise Him that He purposed ahead of time good works for us to do. Praise Him that He knows we are prone to wander and get dirty and made provisions for us through Jesus. Praise God for confession, repentance, and cleansing. Praise Him for Life!

PRAYERFUL RESPONSE:

Write out a prayer of confession, repentance, and thankful praise.

_____

_____

_____

_____

_____

_____

_____

_____

_____

HOW DEEP ARE YOUR ROOTS

TODAY'S SCRIPTURE REFERENCE:

But his delight is in the Law of the LORD,
and in His Law he meditates day and night.
He will be like a tree firmly planted by streams of water,
which yields its fruit in its season,
and its leaf does not wither;
and in whatever he does, he prospers.
Psalm 1:2-4 NASB

A strange thing happened one weekend—a tall, stately, beautiful oak tree just keeled over. It was a lovely, sun-shiny day with no wind or rain. It fell to the ground while the man who owned the yard was mowing in a different area. It was a blessing he was not mowing in that area at that moment!

It was quite a shock to him! It was a shock to the neighborhood, too, because the tree had appeared to be healthy and strong enough to withstand strong winds for many years to come. I am not an arborist, but after speaking with the owner and hearing his observations, it appears that the drought had taken a terrible toll on that tree. Its roots were dry, brittle, and shallow.

Evidently, the outside of the tree was surviving on what had been stored in the trunk, giving the leaves and branches the appearance of a robust, hearty condition. Yet, all the while, the tree was not flourishing at all; it was slowing dying due to lack of water. It made me recall Psalm 1.

> *Blessed is the person who does not walk in the counsel of the wicked, nor stand in the path of sinners, nor sit in the seat of scoffers! But his delight is in the law of the LORD, and on His law he meditates day and night. He will be like a tree planted by streams of water, which yields its fruit in its season, and its leaf does not wither; and in whatever he does, he prospers.*
> Psalm 1:1-3 NASB

I don't want to be a tree that keels over due to lack of water! Let us be individuals who deeply engage with the Word, quenching our souls' thirst with its "waters." Let us put our roots deep down into His truths that will anchor our lives to the One Who is our Living Hope (1 Peter 1:3)!

Jesus has imputed His righteousness onto us (1 John 4), and we learn to practice living out that righteousness through the instructions in His Word. Consider this precious Psalm:

The righteous person will flourish like the palm tree, He will
grow like a cedar in Lebanon. Planted in the house of the
LORD, They will flourish in the courts of our God.
They will still yield fruit in advanced age; They will be full of
sap and very green, to declare that the LORD is just; He is
my Rock, and there is no malice in Him.
Psalm 92:12-15 NASB

I'm going to date myself here, but here's a quote from the movie *Back to the Future:* "Let's make like a tree and leaf." I saw you roll your eyes! Ha!

Let's not leave; instead, let us put down deep roots into the love and Word of God so that we flourish even in high winds, yielding fruit and bringing glory to the One who is the Giver of everything good!

PRAYERFUL RESPONSE:

How can you deepen your roots so that you bear much fruit for God's Kingdom? What specific steps can you take?

_____

_____

_____

_____

_____

_____

_____

_____

HOW THEN ARE WE TO LIVE?

TODAY'S SCRIPTURE REFERENCE:

Do not conform to the pattern of this world.
Romans 12:2 NIV

O ne semester, I took a master's level course on the book of Judges. Let me tell you, it was not easy, as Judges is a hard book to read. It is full of deceit, bloodshed, faithlessness, suffering, injustice, and the downward spiral of God's people into the abyss of sin and rebellion against the One who loves them faithfully.

Our study focused on the pattern of Israel's relationship with God:

1. They do evil and worship the gods of the people around them.
2. God uses the people around them to discipline/bring them back.
3. The people cry out to God to deliver them.
4. God raises up a judge to deliver them from their enemy.
5. They live in peace while the judge is alive, then fall into greater evil than before!

We observe two things in this cycle. The first is the faithlessness of the people of Israel and their inability to keep a covenant with God. Instead of becoming a people who proclaim God to the nations around them, they acclimate to those very nations God told them to conquer. They adopted their customs and gods and married their daughters and sons. Rather than nations discovering the one true God, Israel becomes "Caanan-ized!"

The second thing we see is the faithfulness and grace of our God. Over and over, we see His lovingkindness extended to His chosen people as He disciplines them with their enemies only to rescue them when they cry out to Him for deliverance. Even in the face of their rebellion and breaking of the covenant, He is faithful to them and to His covenant.

As the book of Judges draws to its conclusion, we see a stark warning against adapting our behavior to the world around us. In Jesus, we are holy, and we are called to live holy lives because it is written: "Be holy as I am holy" (1 Peter 1:15-16NIV).

So how, then, are we to live practically? How do we live walking in the grace and holiness we are called to instead of adapting to the world like the Israelites did? I suggest we begin with 1Peter 1:13-19, readying our hearts and minds for action through obedience out of love for all our Father has done for us through Jesus.

It's crucial to start doing this at home. In obedience and in holiness, we are to love all our church family, locally and globally, fervently from the heart. Loving fervently is a choice. It shows grace and gives up our need to be right in exchange for being kind and forgiving. We must realize that we are all "goobers" capable of any sin at any moment. It's common for all of us to do foolish things that hurt others.

Loving is responding rather than reacting and apologizing when you don't get it right. Loving is having conversations that may not always lead to agreements or total reconciliation, but certainly forgiveness and understanding.

We can't deny it; people are messy. God put messy people together in a congregation under His Spirit and said, "Be one in me and in my Father. Let the world see how much you love one another so they will believe in me." That can be a tall order but for grace.

Grace is a kindness granted, a benefit, a favor done without expectation of return. God's grace is His unconditional love and kindness towards mankind, given without any deserving or earning on our part. Considering the grace that has been extended to each of us, as we yield to His Spirit within us, we live in and offer that grace to our brethren. After all, He has set us apart to do just that for the rest of the world. Let us be holy; through the power of His own Spirit, He enables us to do so.

Let us not live as the Israelites did, adapting to and reacting to the culture around them. Let us respond with and reflect the grace, love, and kindness of the image of the One in whom we were re-created.

PRAYERFUL RESPONSE:

In what ways have you adopted the ideas and culture of the world? What can you do to align yourself with a Biblical view rather than a worldview?

_____

_____

_____

_____

_____

_____

_____

_____

_____

HUMILITY

TODAY'S SCRIPTURE REFERENCE:

He leads the humble in what is right,
and teaches the humble his way.
Psalm 25:9 ESV

A while ago, I did a topical study on humility, and it struck me like a slap in the face that I ain't got it! There are periods of time when I do acts of humility, serving other people when it's inconvenient or when I'd rather be doing something else.

However, upon closely examining the initial scripture in the study (Philippians 2), I discovered that humility has greater depth. Humility begins with how I view God. Is He who He says He is or not? If He is, then all I think, say, and do must revolve around what He thinks, says, and does.

The definition of humility is a posture of the heart and mind characterized by the absence of pride and self-importance. It's a commitment to the well-being of others. For the believer, it is recognizing your dependence on the Lord and willingly submitting to His authority and rule over your life. Considering all that He is, it is a deep sense of how little we are.

Humility is the core of the Christian life. To believe that Jesus is our Savior, we must first humble ourselves to the point that we recognize our need for a Savior. Through humility, we walk in obedience, bowing our will to His. Humility is the foundation upon which kindness, compassion, gentleness, mercy, self-control, patience, joy, and peace are built.

Humility is submission. Philippians 2:5-11 gives us the most beautiful description of the humility and submission of Christ on our behalf. He set the example for us, His disciples. Jesus knows what it feels like to give things up for the sake of others. He stands ready and waiting to help us when we struggle to do so (Hebrews 4:15-16). When we humble ourselves and submit to Him, we join forces with the one who can assist us in defeating pride and sin.

Here's the thing that got me: Because we do have the encouragement of Christ, His love, fellowship with the Spirit, and His affection and mercy, we can think like Christ. We can humble ourselves before him and others. Humbling ourselves before Him is not an option; it is a command.

The sad reality for me and others like me is that we are not taking His Word seriously. We consider this a stark suggestion instead of an absolute command. We are not humbling ourselves before Him if we still want to do things our way or when His way is convenient. If we don't see His Word as the ultimate authority of our lives, then we are placing ourselves above Him. Humility begins with how I view God. Is He the sovereign Lord, King of kings, Immanuel, Creator, God of your life or not?

There's a very good reason why God asks us to humbly submit to Him. Philippians 2:14-15 says it is so that we will shine as lights in the world. We cannot shine as lights in the world if our lives look exactly like everyone else's. We humbly submit to God's commands so the world will see Him in us and be saved.

PRAYERFUL RESPONSE:

How "shiny" are you? The key to your sparkle is humility. That's walking in obedience. In what areas is the Holy Spirit showing you your lack of humility?

_____

_____

_____

_____

_____

_____

_____

_____

_____

HUMMING RIGHT ALONG

TODAY'S SCRIPTURE REFERENCE:

*Out of his fullness we have all received grace in place of
grace already given.*
John 1:16 NIV

As I've mentioned before, watching the hummingbirds as they flit this way and that around our feeders and flowers in our yard is something I quite enjoy. With their tiny wings beating, they hover and hum, their little green bodies shimmering in the sun, making them incredibly cute. So cute—except when they're not!

They can be so tyrannical and downright mean as they fuss and fight with each other over the sugar water in the feeders. Each one seems to think the four feeders are only for them. They don't realize that Glenn and I have an abundant supply of both sugar and water and that we will happily keep the feeders full for all to get their fill!

If we are not careful, we can be like the hummingbirds. We can let fear and self-preservation take over our hearts and hoard the very gifts our Father has given us from His never-ending abundant supply (Philippians 4:19).

Remember the toilet paper fiasco during the COVID-19 pandemic? Guilty. What a terrible thing to run out of, though, right? You must admit that we are experts at justifying our selfishness, ingratitude, and lack of generosity. That is because we live our lives oblivious to the truth that God owns everything and is the giver of everything we have, need, or want.

The hummingbirds are focused on one thing: eating! They must fuel up for their long flight to Mexico, and that motivates their actions. What about you and I? What is our focus?

The Bible teaches us that what we believe drives our emotions and actions. That is why God has addressed the mind so often in His Word. Romans 12:2 instructs us to have our minds renewed and be transformed, so that we can understand God's will and what is good, acceptable, and perfect. In Philippians 4:8, Paul tells us specifically what things to think about: things that are true, just, pure, lovely, commendable, excellent, and worthy of praise.

How will you know what these things are? How can you train your mind to create an environment for the Holy Spirit to do His work of transformation? Study. Meditate on His Word. Philippians 4:9 ESV, which follows the list of things to think about, Paul says, "What you have learned and received and heard and seen in me— practice these things and the God of peace will be with you."

We learn what is true, pure, and lovely as we study. We grow as we meditate and apply what we study. The Holy Spirit transforms us as we yield to Him to teach and guide us.

How magnificent is the sight I see in my head when I read Galatians 5:25 ESV, which says, "If we live by the Spirit, let us also keep in step by the Spirit." The Greek word used here means to march in step, as in a military line. Do you see the picture? You, me, and all other believers linked arm and arm with the Holy Spirit, walking in step. Unified while studying His Word, listening to His teachings and promptings, and being guided in the will of the Father. Maybe even humming a catchy tune. Much different from the hummingbirds!

PRAYERFUL RESPONSE:

It's "confession" time: List ways you behave like the hummingbirds.

_____

_____

_____

_____

_____

_____

_____

_____

_____

Ask the Father in prayer to keep your heart soft and your ears open so you can hear His Spirit when He guides you to "Walk this way."

HUNGER GAMES

TODAY'S SCRIPTURE REFERENCE:

Blessed are those who hunger and thirst for righteousness,
for they will be filled.
Matthew 5:6 NIV

Over the years, we have picked different themes for our annual Cousins Camp. Themes have included ideas like Survivor, Duck Dynasty, Disney, Summer Olympics, and Jurassic World, to mention a few. The games, food, decorations, and camp scripture always match the theme. The older girls decided on the theme Hunger Games for our 12th annual camp in July 2023.

Now, my sister and I did not want to be known as the grandmothers who taught their grandchildren how to kill each other in the arena. So, we had to think long and hard about the games and decided they would revolve around two concepts:

- ✓ Training for battle in the arena.
- ✓ Conducting games and challenges that taught awareness of things to avoid in the arena.

Participants had so much fun learning to shoot with bows and arrows. They had to participate in a scavenger hunt to locate items essential for their survival in the arena. The children collaborated, guiding blindfolded teammates through our simulated "minefields," trusting their team to prevent any mishaps.

Our scripture for the events was:

Blessed are those who hunger and thirst AFTER
righteousness, for they will be filled.
Matthew 5:6 NIV [Emphasis added]

May those kids have a strong desire for God's words and ways, and may they actively seek righteousness in Jesus.

Living a life for Jesus is like living in that arena, and one must be prepared for battle because there are minefields Satan sets up, temptations, and choices. Many life situations can "blow up" our faith, witness, peace and joy, and confidence in Jesus' work on the cross.

Ephesians 6 teaches us how to prepare for spiritual battles by putting on the full armor of God. Each piece of armor has a specific role in our pursuit of righteous living.

- ✓ We wear the **belt of truth** so that we can discern good from evil.
- ✓ We wear the **breastplate of righteousness** around our hearts for protection from a death blow.
- ✓ We put on the **shoes that give us peace** with God through His Gospel.
- ✓ He hands us the **shield of faith** to extinguish all the lies of the evil one.
- ✓ Lastly, we put on the **helmet of salvation**, which protects our minds as we seek to think and, thus, behave like Christ.

Our weapon of choice is the Word of God, which is "God-breathed and is useful for teaching, rebuking, correcting and training in righteousness" (2 Timothy 3:16 NIV).

All of us are in training for battle. Our righteousness grows when we wear His armor and stand firm in His promises. We wear our armor and rely on God's promises so that we "may be thoroughly equipped for every good work" (2 Timothy 3:17 NIV).

In the arena of life, we always seek His will and protection by covering our armor in prayer. I pray that you will put on your armor and train well!

PRAYERFUL RESPONSE:

What steps are you taking to actively train yourself in righteousness? Is there anything you need to incorporate into your routine, like daily prayer, attending church, helping others, or meditating and studying His word? Are there any hazards you should be wary of while navigating the arena?

_____

_____

_____

_____

_____

_____

_____

_____

_____

IN HIS TIME

TODAY'S SCRIPTURE REFERENCE:

There is a time for everything,
and a season for every activity under the heavens.
Ecclesiastes 3:1

My mother, Jackie Boswell, passed away on January 6, 2022; she was with us for 92 blessed years. She had been living with Glenn and me in the months leading up to Christmas that year. Since I had a full house for the holidays, she went home with my sister, Becky, after her last hospital stay. After being there for only a week, she went to be with Jesus.

One day, when my mother was here with us, we were both kind of mopey because she was having so much trouble breathing. Every time she attempted to walk across the room, she had to stop and catch her breath. In my quiet time, I whined a little to the Lord about it, and He sweetly reminded me of all the ways He *had* and *was* blessing us during this time together.

Mother and I had a discussion about it, and she smiled up at me because she was somewhat petite. She said, "In His time. He does *everything* in His time."

Reflecting on that precious moment we shared, hugging and expressing gratitude for His protection, I wonder if Mother pondered all the "In His times" in her life.

In His time, He broke through to the heart of her alcoholic husband, my father, forever changing the trajectory of our family's spiritual direction. Mother realized that Jesus died for her personally, not just for the whole world, and one by one, I, my sister, and my brother were saved.

In His time, our parents faithfully served in the church, working with children. Mother was a Sunday School teacher, and Daddy worked with R.A.s. Many lives were impacted by their love for Jesus.

In His time, they both followed God's call into full-time ministry as camp managers for Zephyr Encampment when they were in their fifties. This move impacted our whole family as each grandson worked as a staffer, serving the Lord and growing spiritually. God blessed our family greatly, as well as countless children who went to camp over the sixteen years they served there.

In His time, God called them to help plant a church at Lake Tawakoni when they moved back to Greenville. Daddy led the music, and Mother played the piano. They both taught children, R.A.s and G.A.s, and Daddy taught adult Sunday School.

In His time, God called Daddy home, and though she was sad, Mother was comforted. This was taped to her bathroom mirror: "If we're willing, God is our song when we are happy, our escape when we are tempted, our hope when we're despairing, our joy in tribulation, our strength in weakness, and our immortality in dying. Ultimately, He Himself is our health."

In His time, God healed my mother with His ultimate healing. Now that she is with the Lord, I imagine she can breathe without struggling and enjoy taking walks again. She is reunited with Daddy, our son, Justin, and nephew, Rusty.

Mother and Daddy are singing duets together in Heaven, just like they did here on earth. Their favorite song was by Gordon Jensen, who says, "*It's a song holy angels cannot sing. Amazing grace, how sweet the sound. It's a song holy angels cannot sing. I once was lost, but now I'm found!*"

My Bible study friend reminded me about the importance of patience in trusting God's work in us and for us—in His time. Sometimes, our faith is tested. But God is always with us, walking beside us and in us with His Spirit as we wait for His time. My mother understood that.

In His time, in His time
He makes all things beautiful in His time
Lord, please show me every day
As You're teaching me Your way
That You do just what You say in Your time.

LINDA DIANE BALL

PRAYERFUL RESPONSE:

What is God showing you about "His Time"?

_____

_____

_____

_____

_____

_____

IN TANDEM

TODAY'S SCRIPTURE REFERENCE:

It is the Lord who goes before you.
Deuteronomy 31:8 NIV

Several years ago, Glenn and I bought a tandem bicycle at an estate sale. It needed a little work, so he found a bike shop that could find the parts it needed. As we rode that bike down our country lanes, we received smiles, stares, and waves. The most fun was watching the grandkids ride. Of course, the level of enthusiasm varies between the different personalities as we have ten grandchildren.

When Kadin and Kaitlyn ride, there is always a debate as to who will ride in front. It can be a lengthy discussion because the front person is in charge. They are in control of steering and braking. Kadin and Kaitlyn both like to be the boss, deciding what lane to turn down, how fast to go, and when to stop. As you can imagine, getting started takes them a little while.

On the other hand, Seth is an easy-going fellow who doesn't mind sitting back and letting someone else take the wheel. He is perfectly content to go along for the ride. Abigail is more like Kadin and Kaitlyn. She ends up at the controls when riding with Khloe or Zoe. These three are also good about taking turns.

How about you? Would you be more comfortable steering and being responsible for where the bike goes, how fast, and for the person behind you? Or would you prefer to let someone who feels more confident do the decision-making while you pedal along? Whichever works, it is fun to watch two people working together in tandem and having fun doing it.

It takes both kinds of people to make the bike work. Someone is in charge and willing to pedal, yet yielding his will to the other. Of course, I haven't met a backseat rider who didn't try to help with navigation.

Thinking along these lines, I asked myself, "Am I riding in tandem with the Holy Spirit in the front seat or the back? God chose us to be saved through the sanctifying work of the Spirit and our belief in the truth (2 Thessalonians 2:13). The Spirit teaches us, disciplines us, guides us in all wisdom and understanding, prays for us, and comforts us. He can't do that very well if we decide to control things and steer the bike.

You see, God gave us His Spirit so that we would walk in step with Him or pedal with Him, so to speak. In Galatians, Paul teaches that when we live in the Spirit by allowing Him to guide our thinking and behaving, we will not gratify the sins of the flesh. Rather, we will exhibit His nature of love, joy, peace, patience, kindness, goodness, faithfulness, gentleness, and self-control (Galatians 5). We cannot do that from the front seat. Our will must be yielded to His.

As we allow Him to "ride in front," He brings us to the place where His desires become our own. He fills us up with Himself so that we can understand what the will of the Lord is (Ephesians 5:17-18). The Gift of the Holy Spirit is for our edification, encouragement, peace, and comfort.

Living in tandem with Him, we trust Him to steer our "bikes," and we do our share of the pedaling. Oh yes! We work alongside Him in the sanctification process. Together, the Spirit transforms us into the likeness of Jesus as we discipline ourselves to stay committed to God and His Word.

Bike riding requires effort, but it is also enjoyable. It has the added benefit of keeping us fit and in better health. Riding in tandem with the Holy Spirit is also work. It is not easy to die to yourself each day. It is also fun as we see Him gradually growing us to be like Jesus, making us spiritually healthy.

PRAYERFUL RESPONSE:

Are you riding in the front seat or back seat with the Holy Spirit? Why is it difficult for you to give up control and trust Him? In what ways do you try to be the "navigator"? Pray, asking God to guide, teach, and help you yield your will to His.

_____

_____

_____

_____

_____

_____

_____

_____

IT'S OK TO BE A WEIRDO

TODAY'S SCRIPTURE REFERENCE:

*Do not be conformed to this world, but be transformed
by the renewal of your mind, that by testing you may discern
what is the will of God, what is good
and acceptable and perfect.*

Romans 12:2

Being unable to read a daily Bible passage without pausing multiple times to search for Greek definitions or related scriptures could be a sign of being a Bible weirdo. Yep! Something that should only take about 10 minutes can quickly turn into 35 in a New York minute! *It's a good thing I am retired!* I can't be the only one who gets excited about finding gems within the treasure chest of God's Word!

Recently, I was finishing up the book of Philippians and discovered something I had never noticed in this passage before—how to stand firm in the Lord. In Ephesians, I read about the importance of putting on the armor of God to stand against the devil's schemes. Four different times in Ephesians 6:10-18, Paul admonishes Christians to stand dressed in:

- God's belt of truth,
- His breastplate of righteousness,
- the shoes of Gospel of peace, and
- His helmet of salvation, taking up the shield of faith, and
- The sword of the Word, praying at all times.

In the final chapter of his letter to the Philippians, Paul encourages us to stay committed to the Lord, continue making progress, and have the mindset of Christ (2:5). Here's where I got excited. Beginning in 4:4, Paul gives practical instructions on standing in the Lord. We stand firm by the following:

- Rejoicing in the Lord always!
- Being reasonable with everyone,
- Giving our requests to God with thanksgiving rather than being anxious and worried.

As we pray, trusting in Him, He gives us His peace that no one understands yet guards our hearts and minds (and keeps us sane!). We should contemplate His thoughts, His truths, and what is honorable, just, pure, lovely, and commendable. We think about what is worthy of praise—HIM!

You see, I'm facing a problem, and I'm probably not the only one. My thoughts and behaviors are often driven by my feelings. If my thoughts, feelings, and behaviors are not aligned, I am not standing firm with His thoughts.

That's when I pray, asking my Father to let His Word of truth wash over my mind, transforming my thoughts to think like Christ. Aligning my thoughts, feelings, and actions with His allows me to stand firm in the Lord.

I pray that each of us will spend time with the Lord in submission to Him and to His Word. He will transform us into disciples who stand firm with Christ and separate from the world—standing in His peace, contentment, reasonableness, thanksgiving, and joy. The world may look at us like we're weirdos, but that's okay. Jesus said that as we love Him and each other, the world will see Him in us. Maybe they will want to be weirdos, too.

PRAYERFUL RESPONSE:

Of the four ways listed to stand firm, which is easiest and hardest for you? Pray, asking the Lord to transform your thoughts and actions to reflect His Word.

_____

_____

_____

_____

_____

_____

_____

_____

KEEP YOUR HEAD STRAIGHT

TODAY'S SCRIPTURE REFERENCE:

For as he thinketh in his heart, so is he.
Proverbs 23:7 KJV

L et's be honest. Occasionally, I find myself in a funk, feeling bland, blah, and flat. Yes, that's the word—flat. I don't like it when I feel that way because, you know, it's like living in a black-and-white world. Life goes on, and you go on, but the "yippy skippy" is not in your step!

I wallowed like that for a day, then thought, *"Wait a minute! This is not how the Lord intended me to feel. What am I always teaching others to do?"* That's when I realized (again!) that there is no point in knowing the truth if you don't apply the truth in the nitty-gritty of life!

So, I whipped out my Thankful List, carefully and prayerfully reading through all the spiritual, material, and emotional blessings that are mine, simply because God is good, loving, gracious, and kind. I didn't get far down the list before my "moody feelings" turned into gratitude as I confessed to Him my thoughts of wandering from His presence and truths.

For me, that is where the battle is fought—for my mind. Satan knows my tendency to overthink, assume, envy, seek my own glory, and want my own way. Peter says the devil is like a lion, ready to pounce and attack us in our weak areas to destroy us, our witness, our joy, and peace (1 Peter 5:8-9).

But our God knows us better! He knows a thought before it's even formed. The Word instructs us to hold our thoughts captive in Christ to resist Satan's schemes (Romans 12:1-2). By feasting on The Word and having other safety nets in place (like a Thankful List), we can rein in those rebellious thoughts, bringing them into submission to Christ.

Here's the deal, Lucille. You must be ready and alert. Do you know how to analyze your thinking? The Bible clearly shows us that our thoughts and beliefs drive our feelings and actions. What you think and believe directly affects how you feel and act.

So, when your feelings are out of whack for seemingly no reason, take a moment to think about your thinking! What have your thoughts been revolving around? If you can identify a lie or assumption, go to scripture to find the truth.

For example, take a break if you have spent too much time listening to negative news. Create boundaries for yourself regarding how much you believe you can handle. If a situation in your life leads you to overwhelming thoughts, try keeping scripture cards handy. Memorizing and meditating on His promises personally aided me when I struggled with anxiety. They were in my purse, ready to be used whenever necessary.

These are worrisome times. Sometimes, it seems like everyone is upset with each other for something. I'm grateful I don't get in a funk more often! Paul wrote to Timothy, telling him not to be anxious because God had not given him a spirit of fear but a sound mind.

And do you know what? We, too, have sound minds. 1 Corinthians 2:16 says that we have the mind of Christ! I don't think you can get any sounder than that, do you? Let's keep that in mind, and I bet that will keep our heads straight!

PRAYERFUL RESPONSE:

Write the things you are thankful for. Use the list as a reminder of your blessings when you're feeling low.

_____

_____

_____

_____

_____

_____

_____

_____

KEEPY UPPY

TODAY'S SCRIPTURE REFERENCE:

Rejoice in the Lord always. I will say it again: Rejoice! Let
your graciousness be known to everyone. The Lord is near.
Don't worry about anything, but in everything, through
prayer and petition with thanksgiving, let your requests be
made known to God. And the peace of God, which surpasses
every thought, will guard your hearts and your minds in
Christ Jesus. Finally brothers, whatever is true, whatever is
lovely, whatever is commendable . . .
dwell on these things.
Philippians 4:4-8 HCSB

My grandson Baxley, or Bax as I call him, has a favorite game called "Keepy Uppy." All you need to play this game is a balloon, preferably a yellow one. There is only one rule in this game: don't let the balloon touch the ground at any cost!

This sounds like a simple, safe game for a Granna to play, right? Tell that to the bruise on my left arm! You see, we competitive people, in our efforts to keep the balloon up, sometimes trip over our partners, obstacles, or even our own stinkin' feet!

Lately, I have been in a little bit of a dry spell. On my walk this morning, the Lord reminded me of this fun time with Bax and how it applies to me. Like a balloon, there are times when I feel this way. Whether the circumstances around me, my negligence of my time with Him, or my own negative thinking, I am being "bopped" around in the air.

But I will never be blown away or completely fall to the ground because I am tethered to the unchangeable, faithful Rock of Ages. My emotions may fly all over the place, and circumstances knock me here and there, but He has hold of me. I am grounded by His great name, who He is, and what He does.

The second thing He revealed is that I sometimes try to play "keepy uppy" on my own. Have you ever tried to play that game alone? It's hard to keep the balloon off the ground without a partner. It's also not nearly as much fun!

Baxley and I laugh so much when we play together, even when we mess up and the balloon falls. We just pick it up and start over. And if it pops, we blow up another one!

Oh, how much joy and laughter we miss out on when we try to live our everyday lives on our own without relying on our partner, the Holy Spirit. It is exhausting to play life in your own strength. His grace is so abundant, free, and sufficient for everything you are trying to "keepy uppy."

The comforting thing is that when we let life's balloons fall, He is faithful to forgive and extend mercy, grace, and forgiveness. Sometimes, He shows us that certain balloons in life can be dropped.

The only thing I really want to "keepy uppy" is my relationship with Him, eliminating the stress of the balloon game and focusing on Him. I need to keep my eyes on Him, lean into Him and His

Word, rest in His promises, and trust in His character. When I do this, He and I will soar.

PRAYERFUL RESPONSE:

Recall moments when you felt tossed around by your circumstances like a balloon. Reflect on Philippians 4:6-8 and consider how these verses can help you find peace and regain focus.

_____

_____

_____

_____

_____

_____

_____

_____

_____

KNOWING JESUS

TODAY'S SCRIPTURE REFERENCE:

Indeed, I count everything as loss because of the surpassing worth of knowing Christ Jesus my Lord.
Philippians 3:8 ESV

Is there someone in your life whom you know so well you can finish each other's sentences? Do you know their favorite ice cream flavor, color, and movie? Or exactly which buttons to push to irritate or to make them laugh?

How did you get to know this person so well? Obviously, by spending a lot of time together. You talk about what you think and how you feel about what is happening in your life and theirs. You share with them what you believe, and you listen to their beliefs and concerns. You have an intimate relationship with this person and develop a love for them, whether it be a friend's love or a romantic love for a spouse or boyfriend.

How well do you want to know Christ? The following scripture expresses how Paul longed to know Christ:

*For His sake, I have suffered the loss of all things and count
them as rubbish, in order that I may gain Christ and be
found in him, not having a righteousness of my own that
comes from the law, but that which comes through faith in
Christ, the righteousness from God that depends on faith—
that I may know him and the power of his resurrection, and
may share his sufferings, becoming like him in his death,
that by any means possible I may attain the resurrection
from the dead.*

Philippians 3:8b-11 ESV

Wow! Is my desire to know Jesus above all? Do I consider everything as "rubbish" or garbage compared to my relationship with Christ? Paul established that his knowing Christ included gaining and being found in Him. Through faith, we come to know Him as His righteousness is imputed upon us by His resurrection. As we share in His life, which includes suffering for His sake, we grow in our faith and come to know Him more.

Just like our other relationships, this one needs our attention. There are many loving ways in which we can grow in our knowledge and friendship with Jesus. The most important ones include spending time with Him in prayer and study of His Word. As we do this, He shows us how to walk with Him in loving submission and obedience. The more we walk with Him, the more we love Him and want to know Him.

In the first chapter of Colossians, Paul tells us that Jesus is before all things and holds all things together. He is the head of the church because of the resurrection and must have first place in our lives. Through Him, all things in heaven or earth are reconciled to

Himself. Through His death, He has presented us holy and blameless and above reproach before Him.

Out of thankfulness and love, our response to His grace and love must be one of pursuit, worship, and sacrifice. The question posed to us is this: What are you going to do to arrange your life so that you can pursue knowing Jesus like Paul? What do you need to take away from or add to your daily schedule? How does your life look like a living sacrifice (Romans 12:1-2)?

Just the time I feel that I've been caught
in the mire of self,
Just the time I feel my mind's
been bought by worldly wealth.
That's when the breeze begins to blow;
I know the Spirit's call.
And all my worldly wanderings
just melt into His Love.

Oh, I want to know You more,
deep within my soul I want to know You,
Oh, I want to know You,
to feel Your heart and know Your mind.
Looking in Your eyes stirs up within me cries
that say, "I want to know You."
Oh, I want to know You more.

And I would give my final breath
to know You in your death and resurrection.
Oh, I want to know You more.

STEVE GREEN

PRAYERFUL RESPONSE:

What adjustments can you make to your daily schedule to prioritize your relationship with Jesus? Make a plan and commit yourself to following it. He is your reward.

_____

_____

_____

_____

_____

_____

_____

_____

_____

LET IT GO

TODAY'S SCRIPTURE REFERENCE:

*If you abide in my word, you are truly my disciples, and you
will know the truth, and the truth will set you free.*
John 8:31-32 ESV

Fall is a wonderful season. The crispy air and the changing colors of the trees are amazing. I love watching the dancing, twirling leaves as they make their way to the ground. Walking among them and kicking them up with my feet is something I love. I even enjoy the crunchy noises they make as I step on them.

But not Glenn. I know he likes Fall, but he is not a falling leaves fan. In fact, each year, he stands in the middle of the yard, stares up at the trees, and tells the leaves to stay put. Then, he threatens them with bodily harm. He tells them if they come down, he will mow them up, mulch them into tiny pieces, and burn them. They don't listen. They twirl and dance to the ground, anyway.

I think the leaves know this secret. You must let go of the old to put on the new. Jesus put it this way when He talked to the Jews who believed in Him.

Hebrews tells us that Jesus is now our High Priest and has opened for us "through the curtain, that is, through His flesh," a new and living way. Paul instructs us to put off the old self since we have been raised with Christ and now seek the things above. Setting our minds on Christ, we are to put on the new self, "which is being renewed in knowledge after the image of its creator" (Colossians 3:10, NIV).

As I was walking along, kicking up the old leaves, I thought about three things we need to let go of:

- Let go of old ways of thinking so that we can have the mind of Christ. Romans 12:1 tells us the best way to seek things above, over things of this earth, is to be transformed by renewing our minds so that we can discern the will of God.

- Let go of pursuing/desiring many things to desire the one main thing, which is to love Christ above all. Remember the story of Martha and Mary? Sometimes, life gets too crowded with good things, leaving no room for the Best. Simplify your life. Love God. Love people.

- Let go of old sinful habits and practices to walk in the newness of life in the grace of Jesus.

Look carefully then how you walk, not as unwise but as wise,
making the best use of the time, because the days are evil . . .
be filled with the Spirit . . . giving thanks always and for
everything to God, the Father,
in the name of our Lord Jesus Christ,
submitting to one another out of reverence for Christ.
Ephesians 5:15-21 ESV

How can we not rejoice in this new life we've been given? We were in a desperate situation, unable to earn or create our own righteousness. Jesus stepped into our reality and paid our sin debt with grace, fulfilling our dire need. He performed the ultimate miracle, transforming us from the old existence of sin and debt to a new one of grace and life.

Let us thankfully and graciously live unto the new by letting go of the old. The old wasn't that great, anyway.

PRAYERFUL RESPONSE:

What parts of your old life do you need to let go? What will you replace them with that is new in Jesus?

_____

_____

_____

_____

_____

_____

_____

_____

_____

LOVE WITH GRACE

TODAY'S SCRIPTURE REFERENCE:

I pray also for those who will believe in me through their message, that all of them may be one, Father, just as you are in me and I am in you. May they also be in us so that the world may believe that you have sent me.

John 17:20b-21

Allow me to tell you a love story. Nick's wife, Beka, has always had trouble with her back as long as I have known her. But when she was pregnant with their third child (Baxley), it got incredibly worse because the baby had settled on her sciatic nerve. She was in constant, extreme pain. She would lose feeling in her leg, and because of this, there was no way for her to be comfortable or to sleep. Yet, she still took care of her family.

She tried all kinds of treatments, massages, yoga, topical ointments, stretching, and prayers with anointed oil. Undoubtedly, she did all she could to avoid anything that might harm the baby. She and Nick would pray together, crying together over her pain and over that sweet baby growing inside her. Obviously, it was a scary time for them because the doctors were concerned about the long-term effects of the trauma on her back. If anyone could ever have a reason to resent anybody, it would be Beka. She suffered incredible pain for seven months, all the while deeply loving the source of her pain.

When Baxley was born, it was certainly a day of rejoicing. Because of his mother's love and care, he was healthy and, of course, beautiful. The very next day, Beka underwent back surgery.

Now we have a delightful grandson who is so much fun. We can't imagine a world without him. Of course, sometimes his parents have wondered what in the world they are going to do with him! But here's the deal: Love finds a way.

Love brought him into this world, a love that endured so much pain just to get him here. With much grace, love got him through the terrible twos and horrendous threes. Love will carry him on into adolescence and the teens because that is what we do. We love our children.

God loves His children enough to put His own Spirit within us, to strengthen us, empower us, teach us, and guide us to do the impossible. We can choose to love even when it's difficult, and let's face it: It is not always easy to love. Jesus said that we are to love one another, and that is how the world will know that we are His (John 14-15).

John 1:16 says that His Spirit pours out grace upon grace, one blessing after another. That is how we can love each other when we are not so lovable and acting like we are in our "terrible twos!" We respond with grace. How can we, who have been given so much grace by our Father, not extend grace to a fellow believer?

Extending grace means listening instead of judging. We listen to hear the other person's heart, not listen with an agenda so that we can give a rebuttal or argument to prove our point. We may not agree, but we can still find some common ground because we share the same Spirit.

Extending grace means encouraging instead of gossiping. Gracious people are kind. They seek to understand rather than condemn. Loving one another sometimes means enduring them, doesn't it? If it were easy, the world could do it and wouldn't need His disciples to show them the love of Jesus.

We love because He told us to love and showed us how. It's not an option. We love and walk in unity with God the Father, Jesus the Son, and the Holy Spirit, and we walk with each other so that the world may believe (John 17:21). We can only do that by His grace.

PRAYERFUL RESPONSE:

How has God shown His love for you? Who has shown the love of God to you? Who has God laid on your heart to love with grace?

_____

_____

_____

_____

_____

_____

_____

_____

LOVE YOUR BODY

TODAY'S SCRIPTURE REFERENCE:

*For this is the message that you have heard from the
beginning, that we should love one another.*

1 John 3:11 ESV

W hen I look in the mirror, I just don't like certain parts
of me. If truth be told, I wish they would go away, but
at my age, I'm afraid they are here to stay. Beka, my
daughter-in-law, will fuss at me and remind me that I am "fearfully
and wonderfully made," and she is right.

I am His creation, formed in my mother's womb just the way He
planned me to be (Psalm 136). Now, being re-born into His
kingdom through Jesus, I am wrapped up in His righteousness,
totally loved and accepted by Him.

If we're being honest, you've probably met Jesus' followers whom
you don't like. Maybe you even wish they would just go away! But,
as a disciple of Jesus, you do not have that option. You are called
and commanded to love your body.

1 John 3:16,18 ESV tells us, "By this, we know love, that he laid
down his life for us, and we ought to lay down our lives for the
brothers . . . Little children, let us not love in word or talk but in
deed and in truth." Later, in the fourth chapter of 1 John, he tells us

that love is from God because He is love and that everyone who is born of God knows Him and shows love.

Jesus prayed for us, His body. In John 17, he prayed for our unity with Him, the Father, and the Holy Spirit, bound by our love for them and for each other. Paul teaches that we are to be united with the same understanding and conviction and that there should be no divisions among us (1 Corinthians 1:10).

So, even though there may be things about a fellow believer we may not like, we are still to love them, for they too are fearfully and wonderfully made. They are dearly loved by the Trinity, and we are one with them; we are all part of the same Body of Christ.

Does it make sense that one part of your body would try to hurt another part? Would you try to put out your own eye? Or break your own arm? That sounds absurd, doesn't it? When we say hurtful things about fellow believers or undermine their ministry somehow, that's exactly what we are doing to the Body of Christ.

Jesus took it one step further in Matthew 5:21-24. He took it straight to the heart. If we harbor anger, envy, bitterness, or hurt feelings toward a brother or sister in Christ, can we truly love them, or do we judge them and withhold mercy and grace? To love one another as He does, we should show grace and mercy, remembering this is what He shows us.

Sometimes, to love each other well, mending fences is the first thing we must do to love the Body of Christ. Sometimes, praying for the one who annoys us is how we love the Body. If we are honest, most of us need to ask the Father to mend our hearts and give us love for all members of the Body.

1 Corinthians 1:4-9 explains that our body is equipped with every spiritual gift we need as we eagerly wait for the revelation of Christ. Christ strengthens our body, and the Body is called into fellowship

with Jesus by our faithful God. Each member of our congregation is an important part of the Body and is given a spiritual gift so that, together, the Body is equipped to do the work of the Father.

Some are muscles. Some are feet or arms ministering to members of the Body. Some are ligaments holding us together with their prayers and encouraging words. Some are part of the heart with their gift of compassion. Christ is the head, directing, guiding, and lovingly renewing our minds with His Word through the Holy Spirit.

Let us remember to love our body well with all its quirks and hangups. We have the ability to do the most glorious thing on earth together: loving God and loving people. Let us be united in this understanding and conviction.

PRAYERFUL RESPONSE:

How do you effectively show love to the Body of Christ? Is there something you need to do or an attitude you need to adjust to love better?

_____

_____

_____

_____

_____

_____

LOVING HIS WORD

TODAY'S SCRIPTURE REFERENCE:

If Your instruction had not been my delight,
I would have died in my affliction.
I will never forget Your precepts,
for You have given me life through them.
Psalm 119:92-93 HCSB

How important is the Word of God to you? Is it the absolute air you breathe or just words that occasionally inspire you to live your life better? Does it show you the hope that gets you out of bed in the morning and puts a new song in your heart or words that make you happy in the moment?

My prayer for my children and grandchildren is for God to instill a strong longing for His Word in their hearts. And for them to eagerly seek to know Him through studying the Word. I've watched Him answer that prayer in my granddaughter, Kaitlyn, who recently graduated from Texas Tech.

Since her senior year in high school, she has fallen in love with His Word. Now, she regularly meets with other students to study His Word together. It thrills my heart that, as a young woman, she is establishing what I hope will be a lifelong discipline and passion for meeting with the Lord in His Word.

Kaitlyn is discovering how His Word can wash over you like sweet rain, refreshing your soul. Where else will you learn that His faithful love is better than life (Psalm 63:3) or that as you rest in Him, you will not be shaken (Psalm 62:5-8)? When we meditate and study His words, they speak the truth of God to our hearts (2 Timothy 2:15).

> *For the Word of God is living and effective and sharper than*
> *any double-edged sword, penetrating as far as the separation*
> *of soul and spirit, joints and marrow. It is able to judge the*
> *ideas and thoughts of the heart.*
>
> Hebrews 4:12 HCSB

Jesus used the Word of God in His battle against temptation with Satan. Jesus reminded him (and us) that "Man must not live by bread alone but on every word that comes from the mouth of God" (Matthew 4:4 HCSB).

Don't you think our lives are so crowded? We pack our days full within the 24 hours we have. But that's the point, isn't it? It's not our time; it's His.

We are only stewards of the time and life He has given us. As God the Creator, He is the owner of everything (Psalm 50:10-12). We have our origin in Him and are His image-bearers.

Because of the freedom we now have living in His grace through the sacrifice of His Son, Jesus, we are free from sin, death, and condemnation. We can now engage in countless amazing activities. We can love and be loved, know God and be known by Him, and live in grace, mercy, and forgiveness.

Active 1: Now, we can meditate and study His Word freely, driven by our passion, love, and desire for Him and His Word rather than by legalism, duty, or guilt. As we study and apply His truths, He will transform us into the image of His Son as we renew our minds (Romans 12:1-2).

When asked if he wanted to go away with the other disciples who were walking away, Simon Peter told Jesus, "Lord, who will we go to? You have the words of eternal life" (John 6:68 HCSB). The same is true for us. Who else would we go to, and how would we know about Him except through His Word and His Spirit?

My hope is that God helps us become more responsible with our time. This will enable us to connect with Him through His Word and be transformed into His Son's image. His Spirit is already within us to teach and guide us, giving us His fruit to grow and mature as we study and apply what He teaches us.

He has an unlimited supply of grace, knowledge, wisdom, spiritual gifts, guidance, mercy, and forgiveness, just waiting for us to open and receive. He tells us all about it in His Book.

PRAYERFUL RESPONSE:

Ask the Lord to help you find time in your day for Him and His Word. Ask Him to teach you His ways, grow your love for Him and others, and transform you into Jesus' image.

_____

_____

_____

_____

_____

_____

_____

_____

_____

MAJESTY

TODAY'S SCRIPTURE REFERENCE:

The heavens declare the glory of God;
the skies proclaim the work of his hands.
Psalm 19:1 NIV

My sister, Becky, and I enjoy lying on our floaties in the lake. It is very relaxing as you let the gentle breeze rock your boat. Of course, it is not as pleasant when mischievous grandchildren are around to splash and topple you into the water! But one afternoon, there were no children to torment their grandmothers. Undisturbed, Becky and I watched the clouds and imagined the "creatures" we saw in the sky.

The clouds looked like dinosaurs, mermaids, ducks, and grand castles. Then I realized we were gazing into God's majesty. God is majestic over all the earth (Psalm 8:1). Because God has revealed His invisible qualities, His eternal power, and divine nature in His creation, no one has an excuse to deny His existence (Romans 1:20). Our response to His creative genius and awesome power is to be one of awe and thankfulness.

Glenn and I have been blessed to see much of God's majesty in our travels. In Alaska and Canada, we drank in the beauty of grand mountains, blue glaciers, crystal-clear lakes, and incredible waterfalls. We were awed by the beautiful ocean and fragrant floral display in Hawaii.

But in Israel, we walked in the same places Jesus lived, loved, and taught people about our Father. We visited the Mount, where Jesus preached the Beatitudes, and sailed on the Sea of Galilee, where He calmed the storm and walked on water. We felt His majesty as we stood by the open tomb.

John's gospel reveals that Jesus existed from the beginning of the world's creation. So, when we observe this created world and all its glorious splendor, we see the majesty of Jesus.

> *He was with God in the beginning.*
> *Through him all things were made;*
> *without Him nothing was made that has been made.*
> John 1:2-3 NIV

Jesus is the Word made flesh who lived for a while among us. "We have seen his glory, the glory of the one and only Son, who came from the Father, full of grace and truth" (John 1:14 NIV).

The definitions ascribed to "majestic" in Psalm 8 include lofty, excellent, glorious, worthy, famous, and good. According to Jesus, if he were lifted up on the cross, he would gather all people to himself. Hebrews 2:9 (NIV) teaches that Jesus is "now crowned with glory and honor because He suffered death so that by the grace of God He might taste death for everyone." In the fifth chapter of Revelation, we read Jesus is worthy to receive glory, honor, and praise.

All around us is the beauty of His majesty. I see it in my yard's flowers and the clouds overhead. I feel it in the cool breeze on a brisk walk and smell it in the rain. I experience it in the love of my family (even those precocious grandchildren). Jesus stepped into humanity by putting on flesh and blood, but He was, and always will be, majestic. He is worthy of receiving our trust and our allegiance. Furthermore, He is worthy of our praise and gratitude. He is the Son, the second person of the Trinity, who is exalted to the Father's right hand.

Let us worship Him in truth, love, and righteous living. He is worthy of not only our praise but also our lives.

> Majesty, worship His majesty.
> Unto Jesus be all glory and honor and praise!
> Majesty, kingdom authority flow from His throne
> Unto his own; His anthem raise.
> So, exalt, lift up on high the name of Jesus.
> Magnify, come glorify Christ Jesus the King!
> Majesty, worship His majesty.
> Jesus who died, now glorified,
> King of all kings!
>
> JACK HAYFORD

PRAYERFUL RESPONSE:

Take a moment to meditate on the majesty of Jesus, expressing gratitude for who He is and His actions for you. How can you worship Him with your life?

_____

_____

_____

_____

_____

_____

_____

_____

_____

MAY WE NEVER FORGET

TODAY'S SCRIPTURE REFERENCE:

Bless the LORD, O my soul, and all that is within me, bless
his holy name! Bless the LORD, O my soul,
and forget not all his benefits.
Psalm 103:1-2 ESV

Forgetting happens to everyone. We forget the names of people we know or where we put stuff we need. At times, appointments slip our minds. We forget children at the beach. Oh, wait! That is a story for another time; sorry again, Nick!

I have discovered that as I have gotten older, I seem to forget more. (Sorry for the bad news!) My phone, for example, is always in the most interesting places. Additionally, I walk into rooms with a mission in mind, only to have it slip my mind completely!

But there is one thing I want to never forget: The wonder of the cost of my salvation and how wonderful that salvation is. The Martins, a contemporary gospel group, once sang a song called "May We Never Forget." Part of the lyrics go like this:

So let us decide right here,
right now, to refresh our memory
of how it felt to be lost and how it feels to be free!

May we never forget the cross and the blood,
the price that was paid so that we might live.
May we never forget the cost of this love.
He'll never forsake us; He'll always forgive.
May we never, never forget.

GRANT CUNNINGHAM, JOYCE MARTIN MCCULLOUGH,
MATT HEUESMANN

What measures can we take to avoid forgetting this significant matter? How can we ensure that the WONDER of it stays at the forefront of our minds? The book of Romans provides the answer:

Do not be conformed to this age, but be transformed by the renewing of your mind, so that you may discern what is the good, pleasing, and perfect will of God.
Romans 12:2 CSB

Our Father is so good; He knows how forgetful we are. So, He gives us His Word to show us the way!

In this Romans passage, Paul reminds us to surrender ourselves daily at the altar of worship by renewing our minds with His truths. This is to be a continual, ongoing act of sacrifice that we give of ourselves by abiding in Him (John 15). Just be with Him. Rest in Him. Trust and believe Him, even when it is hard because the world says, "That way makes little sense."

Let us remember the cross, the blood, and the love that held Jesus on the cross. Let's not forget to share that sense of wonder with others. It really is an incredibly wonderful truth to live in, wouldn't you say?

PRAYERFUL RESPONSE:

Spend a few minutes with God, expressing gratitude for sending Jesus to take your place and bear your sins on the Cross. Bless the Lord, remembering His benefits.

_____

_____

_____

_____

_____

_____

_____

_____

_____

MIRROR, MIRROR

TODAY'S SCRIPTURE REFERENCE:

Why do you call me "Lord, Lord," and not do what I tell you?
Everyone who comes to me and hears my words and does
them, I will show you what he is like: he is like a man
building a house, who dug deep and laid the foundation on
the rock. And when a flood arose, the stream broke against
that house and could not shake it,
because it had been well built.
Luke 6:46-48 ESV

As I sit on my bed looking out the window onto the Cove of our lake, the water is so still that it looks like a mirror reflecting everything around it. The trees and docks, the blue sky, and big fluffy white clouds can be seen in the water as if another replicate world exists deep down within it.

Luke 6:40 says that a disciple is not above his teacher, but everyone, when fully trained, will be like his teacher. As disciples of Christ, are we like our teacher, mirroring His character and actions?

So, how do I mirror Jesus? He tells us Himself in Luke 6:46-49 when He asks the question, "Why do you call Me 'Lord, Lord' and do not do what I tell you?" He goes on to say that doing His words is like building our house on a firm foundation of rock. Even during storms, the house will stand firm. Jesus, our firm foundation, requires obedience.

Here are a few examples of the character and actions of Jesus:

- ✓ **Jesus spent much of His time talking with His Father.** When He came down from praying, He was filled with the power of the Spirit! (Luke 6:17-19) We mirror His example by praying.
- ✓ **Jesus is compassionate and kind, seeing people's needs.** Even when He was physically tired from lack of sleep, He taught them, fed them, and healed them. When we help others, we follow His example.
- ✓ **Jesus is bold in His love.** He touched a leper. He healed on a Sabbath, knowing the repercussions it would bring even though He is Lord of the Sabbath. Our lives mirror His when we love the unlovable.
- ✓ **Jesus served humbly.** He washed the disciples' feet. Following Him means we practice putting the needs of others above our own.
- ✓ **Jesus is generous;** He gave His very life to redeem sinful man. He gives us His Holy Spirit, who enables us to produce the fruit of kindness, gentleness, patience, love, goodness, and self-control. As we yield our will to His, His Spirit produces this fruit in us and makes us generous.
- ✓ **Jesus is wise and discerning;** He knew the hearts and minds of those who were against Him. He will give us discernment, too, when we ask for it.

So, when people look at your life, what is reflected to them from your "mirror"? Do they see a prayer warrior? Are they able to perceive genuine love through actions rather than just words? Do they witness someone who exhibits generosity and kindness? Can they identify someone who possesses the ability to give wise guidance? Do they see someone who is like their teacher, Jesus?

PRAYERFUL RESPONSE:

How does your life reflect His? In what areas do you seek to mirror Him more?

_____

_____

_____

_____

_____

_____

_____

_____

NO FEAR

TODAY'S SCRIPTURE REFERENCE:

God is our refuge and strength,
an ever-present help in trouble.
Therefore we will not fear, though the earth gives way
and the mountains fall into the heart of the sea . . .
Psalm 46:1-2 NIV

I hope you don't mind indulging a doting grandmother in this devotional. My son, Nick, posted a video of our grandson, Baxley, on Facebook. Bax is careening on his little coaster bike down a small sidewalk hill beside their church, squealing with delight as he rides into his Daddy's waiting arms.

Initially, I laughed at my grandson's antics. One of the Facebook comments was, "He has no fear!" And upon reading the comment, I thought *he is just like his dad was when he was young.* Then I smiled and added my observation to the post: "He has no fear because he trusts his daddy to catch him."

What about us? Do we trust our Daddy, our Abba Father, to catch us? Are we fearless when walking through difficult circumstances, knowing our Father is with us, ready to keep us from tumbling headlong onto the "concrete?" Can we trust Him so completely that fear disappears, and we find joy in the journey with Him, knowing He waits for us at the end?

Fear is a scary emotion. [*Duh!*] Not because that is what it is but because of what it steals from us—our hope, peace, joy, security, trust, faith, contentment, purpose, thankfulness, and even our fun! That is why God addressed fear in His Word 365 times, one scripture reference for each day of the year.

Our Father knows our hearts and minds; He desires us to fill them with His Truths and Himself. His message is clear—He is there to catch us without a doubt. He wants us to know that we need not be afraid, for the Lord, our God, fights for us (Deuteronomy 3:22).

Jesus Himself said, "Do not be afraid; just believe." Jesus also promised us His peace and told us not to let our hearts be troubled or be afraid (John 14:27). Psalm 23:4 says, "Even though I walk through the darkest valley, I will fear no evil, for you are with me; your rod and your staff, they comfort me."

This year, it has felt like the mountains may fall into the sea for me. But what a comfort and sense of security we have, knowing our Abba Father is our present Help. We do not have to fear because our Father, the creator of the universe, has redeemed us and called us by name. We are His! (Isaiah 43:1)

Isaiah 41:8-10 guarantees that our Abba will catch us before we fall because He will strengthen and help us and uphold us with His righteous right Hand.

But you, Israel, my servant, Jacob, whom I have chosen,
you descendants of Abraham my friend,
I took you from the ends of the earth,
from its farthest corners I called you.

I said, "You are my servant; I have chosen you and have not
rejected you. So do not fear, for I am with you; do not be
dismayed, for I am your God. I will strengthen you and help
you; I will uphold you with my righteous right hand."
Isaiah 41:8-10 NIV

Let us stretch our faith muscles and practice letting go of our fear by trusting our Daddy to catch us and even have a little fun with Him on the ride!

PRAYERFUL RESPONSE:

What has fear stolen from you? The antidote for fear is trusting in the character and promises of God. What assurances do you hold onto when fear enters your mind? What truth becomes evident when you meditate on Psalm 37:23?

_____

_____

_____

_____

_____

_____

_____

_____

_____

_____

A PEARL OF GREAT PRICE

TODAY'S SCRIPTURE REFERENCE:

Again, the Kingdom of Heaven is like a merchant in search of fine pearls, who, on finding one pearl of great value, went and sold all that he had and bought it.
Matthew 13:45-46 ESV

One day, I was in such a tizzy—all day. I lost a bracelet that is truly priceless. It wasn't only valuable in dollars and cents, but it had sentimental value because Glenn gave it to me many years ago. The bracelet was a gold James Avery piece featuring butterflies and pearls. We probably won't replace it, given today's gold prices.

I searched high and low, multiple times, in every nook and cranny. My son, Wes, even drove back to Mesquite in lousy weather to see if it had fallen off my wrist in the restaurant where we had eaten the night before. All to no avail; the bracelet was not to be found. It made me sad.

The next morning, I searched for it one last time. Pulling back couches and looking underneath tables, I was reminded of a parable Jesus taught about the Kingdom of God. In Matthew 13: 45-46 ESV, He said, "The Kingdom of heaven is like a merchant in search of fine pearls, who, on finding one pearl of great value, went and sold all that he had and bought it."

Just as I desperately and diligently searched for my bracelet, which in comparison is of little consequence, the Pearl of Great Price is a treasure worth seeking and finding with all our hearts! Sacrificing everything, including ourselves, is worth it for the Kingdom of Heaven.

In the Sermon on the Mount, Jesus instructed us not to lay up for ourselves treasure on earth but instead seek treasure in heaven. He told us that where our treasure is, that is where our hearts will be, too. He also said that if we seek His Kingdom first, all those other things of earth that we need will be provided.

Jesus Himself is our Treasure! As we place our faith and trust in Him, He becomes the Door that leads us into the Kingdom of Heaven, the Pearl of Great Price. He promised that when we search for Him, we will find Him. I may never find that bracelet, but He found me. That is ever so much better!

There was a valuable lesson I've learned in all of this. Everything we go through in this life, whether significant or inconsequential, can lead us to the realization that a relationship with Him is everything we need. He uses even the loss of a bracelet to teach a spiritual lesson, revealing His work in our hearts and minds.

PRAYERFUL RESPONSE:

What personal lesson do you find in Matthew 13:45-46?

_____

_____

_____

_____

_____

_____

_____

_____

PEER MODEL

TODAY'S SCRIPTURE REFERENCE:

Whoever wants to be my disciple must deny themselves and take up his cross and follow Me.
Mark 8:34 NIV

Our youngest grandson was one of two peer models in his preschool class in a special needs school. Baxley's parents were thrilled when he got accepted into the school due to the small classes and learning opportunities.

His mom and I got tickled, though, when we first heard Baxley referred to as a "peer model." We were very familiar with this precocious, imperfect three-year-old, you see. More than once, we have witnessed that cherub's little dimpled face switch from sweet to sour in a matter of seconds! But the teachers at his school love him, and evidently, he is accomplishing exactly what they want him to do: modeling normal three-year-old behavior for children with special needs.

How precious is that? His best friend is not the other peer model but a kid who needs a friend who will play with him and like him just the way he is. Baxley is learning to see people as people and not as someone in a wheelchair or someone who can't speak plainly. He is discovering the art of loving and accepting people unconditionally.

This little three-year-old has made his Granna stop and look at her own attitudes and prejudices about a lot of things. What type of peer model am I, for instance? Whether we like it or not, we are examples for others in our surroundings.

Paul instructed Timothy to "set an example for the believers in speech, in conduct, in love, in faith, and in purity" (1 Timothy 4:12 CSB). As followers of Jesus, we are to be His hands and feet, actively showing His love for others and modeling compassion for their physical and spiritual needs.

Jesus had some radical ideas about how we are to love people! He expects us to pray for and forgive our enemies, those people who deliberately hurt us (Matthew 5:43-44). This is a command, not a "if you feel like it" kind of thing!

He also tells us to do nothing out of selfish ambition or conceit, but in humility consider others as more important than yourselves. Everyone should look out not only for his own interests but also for the interests of others (Philippians 2:3-4 CSB). Jesus calls for us to die to ourselves—to die to our own ideas and desires for what we think our lives should be and follow His life instead (Mark 8:35).

Being a peer model will look different for me than it will for you. God has gifted each of us with different talents, spiritual gifts, opportunities, and positions in life. He is purposeful in everything He does, and so, wherever He has placed you, He has graced you with everything you need to minister to the people around you.

John 1:16 says that from the fullness of His love, we have received grace upon grace! Don't you just love that? Even our imperfections are covered by His grace. He can and will use imperfect people to show His great love to others. As we surrender our hearts each day to Him, He shows us how to love and serve the people He has placed in our lives.

Just like my mischievous little grandson can be a successful peer model in a special needs school, you and I can be successful Jesus Followers in a world that needs Him because of the fullness of His love and grace!

PRAYERFUL RESPONSE:

Where has God placed you to model His love, grace, mercy, and forgiveness? Who is watching your example? Ask His Spirit to guide your thinking, attitudes, and actions.

_____

_____

_____

_____

_____

_____

_____

_____

THE PERFECT HEART

TODAY'S SCRIPTURE REFERENCE:

And I will give you a new heart, and a new spirit I will put within you. And I will remove the heart of stone from your flesh and give you a heart of flesh.
Ezekial 36:26 ESV

My mother had an imperfect heart and had quadruple bypass surgery in 1987. For over 16 years, she and Daddy were camp managers at Zephyr Baptist Encampment. During that time, her heart was subjected to countless stress tests, echocardiograms, pacemaker procedures, heart caths, and even a mild heart attack. Despite this, it faithfully served her for ninety-two years, enabling her to love her God, family, and friends.

You see, even though her *physical* heart was imperfect, God gave her a perfect *spiritual* heart when, as a mother in her thirties, she gave her flawed one to Him.

If you declare with your mouth, "Jesus is Lord,"
and believe in your heart that God raised Him from the
dead, you will be saved. For it is with your heart that you
believe and are justified, and it is with your mouth that you
profess your faith and are saved.
Romans 10:9-10 NIV

Mother did just that—exchanged her flawed, imperfect heart for a perfect one. God took what she offered Him and made it perfect. He made her complete and completely free of flaws or defects through the blood of Jesus. She was free to love Him and to love people with this new heart of flesh (Ezekiel 36:26).

God replaced the "heart of stone," gave her a new heart, and put a new spirit in her. The Holy Spirit enabled her to love God and, in turn, to love and serve others.

She was not alone. When we believe that Jesus died for our sins and was raised from the dead, God gives each of us this new heart. It is a heart filled with His Spirit to share His love, kindness, peace, comfort, generosity, mercy, grace, and forgiveness with those in our sphere of influence. For most of us, that starts with our family, our first mission field.

Let us love and serve them with our "perfect" hearts; knowing His Spirit within us enables us even in our mess-ups! Rest in His Perfect Heart, His Gift to you.

Bless the Lord who reigns in beauty;
Bless the Lord who reigns in wisdom and with power.
Bless the Lord who fills my life with so much love,
He can make a perfect heart.
DOTTIE RAMBO AND DONY MCGUIRE

PRAYERFUL RESPONSE:

Set aside a moment to thank God for the miraculous transformation that takes place during salvation. Talk to Him about ways you can love and serve Him.

_____

_____

_____

_____

_____

_____

_____

_____

_____

PLAYING GAMES

TODAY'S SCRIPTURE REFERENCE:

In him we have redemption through his blood, the forgiveness of sins, in accordance with the riches of God's grace that he lavished on us. With all wisdom and understanding . . .

Ephesians 1:7-8a NIV

Once, when our grandson was here, we had a tea party. Baxley is really into Mickey Mouse, so we invited my big stuffed Mickey and Minnie to the party. There was "pretend" tea in our teapot, and Baxley was the perfect host, pouring tea for everyone, including himself and his Granna. We enjoyed many cups of the delightful brew!

While reading the seventh chapter of Luke, I stumbled upon a few verses I had previously overlooked. I've been too absorbed in getting to the next good part of the chapter to notice them. In verses 31-32, Jesus asks what He should compare this generation to. He said they're like children playing pretend games of life. Wait—what?

What is adorable for a toddler becomes ridiculous for an adult. I have a question for both of us: what make-believe games have we been playing instead of embracing the real life Jesus invites us to join Him in?

How about the game called I Have To! Have you ever played that game? It's so exhausting because you are hyper-aware of your every move and thought. Or else you won't be accepted, loved, or feel significant. But, in Christ, this is nothing but a childish game! Because God is pleased to do so, He redeems, forgives, accepts you as His child, and lavishes you with His grace (Ephesians 1:7-8).

Then there's the Play Like game. We should avoid playing this game because it's bad. This is the game where we pretend to be God! We pretend we are in control and that we know everything there is to know about a situation. God alone possesses sovereignty and omniscience. He has given us limited knowledge and limited power and control so that we will depend on and trust Him.

Well-known Christian writer A. W. Tozer puts it this way: "God perfectly knows Himself and, being the source and author of all things, it follows that He knows all that can be known. And this He knows instantly and with a fullness of perfection that includes every possible item of knowledge concerning everything that exists or could have existed anywhere in the universe at any time in the past, or that may exist in the centuries or ages yet unborn."

So that leads me to the game of I Wish, which is a game I play often! That is until I remember who my God is. As I reflect on His character and His promises to me in His Word, I am learning to play a new and better game called I Am Thankful and Content.

Jesus' generation did not believe in Him; they did not join into life with Him because He did not play their games. He died for them and us, allowing us to live a joy-filled life with Him.

God, rich in mercy and full of love for us, made us alive forever in Jesus. For we are His creation, created in Christ Jesus for good works, which God prepared ahead of time so that we should walk in them (Ephesians 1:4-10)! Thankful and Content seems like a game that would be both rewarding and exciting!

PRAYERFUL RESPONSE:

Which game do you play the most: I Have To, Play Like, or I Wish? What do you believe you need to do, become, or desire? How can you become better at the game, Thankful and Content? (see Philippians 4:4-13)

_____

_____

_____

_____

_____

_____

_____

_____

_____

PRUNED BY GOD

TODAY'S SCRIPTURE REFERENCE:

I am the true vine, and My Father is the vinedresser.
Every branch in Me that does not bear fruit, He takes away;
and every branch that bears fruit, He prunes it so that it may
bear more fruit. You are already clean because of the word
which I have spoken to you. Remain in Me, and I in you. Just
as the branch cannot bear fruit of itself but must remain in
the vine, so neither can you unless you remain in Me. I am
the vine, you are the branches; the one who remains in Me,
and I in him bears much fruit,
for apart from Me you can do nothing.
John 15:1-5 NASB

To abide means "to remain; continue in; dwell." Some commentaries say it means to "make my home in." Ultimately, it is when we realize we are desperately dependent on Jesus for all things. As the Vine, He is our life, the air we breathe, the Living Water we drink, the Bread that sustains us because we are only branches that can survive if we stay attached to Him!

As we abide in Him and in His Word, He sustains us with His power, strength, and love. He has put His Spirit within us, which produces love, peace, patience, kindness, goodness, graciousness, self-control, forgiveness, joy, and mercy. He covers us with His grace that is beyond anything we can comprehend!

Because we are branches, sometimes we need to be pruned. He allows us to choose other things rather than abiding, and on any given day, sometimes we do just that—choose other things. He doesn't stop loving us or throwing us under the bus when we mess up.

No, He keeps on loving us and prodding us to loving obedience of confession and letting go of sin. His love leads us to repentance and getting back in step with Him. Sometimes, He does that by pruning.

I found four main reasons a gardener prunes his vines. The first is because the limb is damaged or diseased and would hold back the development of the plant. Is there some cherished sin in your life that needs to be pruned? Cherishing sin is not the same as struggling with sin. When we cherish a sin, we are choosing to love that sin more than God. Cherishing sin in our hearts causes a spiritual disconnect from the Vine.

Second, a weak or damaged limb is a danger to people or property. We have several trees on our property. Glenn carefully prunes the dead limbs because he fears one of them could fall on the head of one of his grandchildren! Is there anything in your life that could damage your testimony about Jesus? Are you harboring unforgiveness or bitterness in your heart that would affect your attitude and graciousness?

Third, pruning may be to make the plant more attractive! Sometimes, God prunes us to make us look more like Christ. He makes us more beautiful in His time.

Finally, the Husbandman prunes to promote flowering and fruiting because as plants grow older, they put more energy into roots and foliage. Pruning stimulates the plant to flower and to make fruit again. Are you root-bound? Is your life just a bunch of foliage with no fragrant flowers or sweet fruit of the Spirit? Is your life a sweet aroma to Him?

He is the only One who can produce good fruit in me; that's His job, not mine. As I abide in Him and He in me, He works in me to do everything He planned and prepared for me from the foundation of the world. So easy and yet so hard for strong-willed people who want to do things their own way, right? I guess that's one reason we need pruning because "apart from Me, you can do nothing."

My prayer, after studying this passage, is that instead of whining and complaining about the pruning process, I would be thankful for it. I will pray that my life is spent abiding in the Vine, knowing how desperately needy I am. Yet, understanding myself, I rely on the process that brings me back to Him whenever I stray.

So, I'll ask Him to keep pruning away to make me more like Jesus, even though I know I won't always like it! And I will thank Him for loving me enough to create a new heart in me and for transforming me into the image of His Son.

PRAYERFUL RESPONSE:

Which of the four reasons for "pruning" apply to you? Pray about your need to abide in the Vine.

_____

_____

_____

_____

_____

_____

_____

_____

PULLING WEEDS

Therefore, God's chosen ones, holy and loved, put on heartfelt compassion, kindness, humility, gentleness, and patience, accepting one another and forgiving one another if anyone has a complaint against another. Just as the Lord has forgiven you, so you must also forgive.
Colossians 3:12-13 HCSB

I'm a weed-puller. My mamma was a weed-puller. She would spend hours sitting on her front lawn, pulling up clover and other weeds. She never got them all, and I never will either.

Let me explain: I have a dozen flower beds. Yep, you heard me right. What was I thinking? For one thing, I was ten years younger! You may be wondering where this story is headed.

As usual, God seems to talk to me most often when I'm walking. I was passing a neighbor's flower bed that was full of a variety of pretty flowers. The problem is you can barely see the flowers for the weeds! I thought to myself, "They need to pull those weeds! I could help them, but I have too many of my own to pull!" Almost immediately, it struck me. Yepper. Jesus made a big deal about that!

It is so easy for us to see the weeds in someone else's spiritual garden while totally ignoring the ones in our own! In Matthew 7:1-

7, Jesus discusses how we are to deal with our own sin rather than judge the sin of others. He cautions us:

> *Judge not, that you not be judged. For with the judgment you pronounce, you will be judged, and with the measure you use it will be measured to you.*
> Matthew 7:1-2 ESV

He goes on to say that we first need to take care of our own bigger sin, then we can see "clearly to take the speck out of your brother's eye." He warns us to be cautious about the people we associate with and the ones we confess our sins to.

Our task is to serve as "fruit inspectors." We are told in other scriptures to encourage one another to do good works. It would be silly and even disobedient for us to ignore blatant and willful sin. In Titus 2:4-5 ESV, for example, older women are to teach the younger ones to "love their husbands and children, to be self-controlled, pure, working at home, kind, and submissive to their husbands, so that the word of God may not be reviled."

How can an older woman know what a younger woman needs if she hasn't done a little "fruit inspecting"? One of the most loving things one believer can do for another is to encourage and guide them to confess the sin that they have observed in the other's life. That's fruit inspecting, not judging. Judging is when you see someone's sin and think to yourself, "That is horrible. I'm not like that. I'm better than that. I would never do that!"

The truth is this: "Once you were alienated and hostile in your minds because of your evil actions. But now He has reconciled you by His physical body through His death, to present you holy, faultless, and blameless before Him". (Colossians 1:21-22 HCSB)

Verse 7 tells us that once we walked in sexual immorality, impurity, lust, evil desire, and greed. Praise God for His Grace, Mercy, and Salvation; we are new creations in Christ!

Remembering the truth of who we were, what we were capable of, and who we are NOW in Christ Jesus should leave us so thankful and full of joy that there is no room for judgment! Our thankful hearts are then drawn to "put on heartfelt compassion, kindness, humility, gentleness, and patience, accepting one another and forgiving one another if anyone has a complaint against another." (Colossians 3:12-13 HCSB)

As our love for Jesus grows, we seek to obey Him more, pulling up the "weeds" the Spirit reveals in the soil of our own hearts. Then, as we mature in our faith, He gives us discernment, kindness, and compassion to be "fruit inspectors" to lead others to do the same "weed pulling" in their own hearts. (We tend to recognize the same sin in others that we ourselves have struggled with.)

Colossians 3:16 HCSB tells us to "Let the message about the Messiah dwell richly among you, teaching and admonishing one another in all wisdom, and singing psalms, hymns, and spiritual songs, with gratitude in your hearts to God." Then, in verse 17, Paul tells us to do everything in the name of the Lord Jesus. This is the way we act as "fruit inspectors"...teaching, admonishing, loving, doing everything in His name and for His glory, and allowing others to inspect our "fruit" in the same way!

This way, the only One sitting in the judge's seat is The Judge Himself, The Lord God Almighty. Only the Creator has the right to judge His creation.

Don't sit in His chair.

PRAYERFUL RESPONSE:

What is the difference between judging and "fruit inspecting"? How can you stay out of God's chair and let Him do the judging?

_____

_____

_____

_____

_____

_____

_____

_____

PURSUIT OF HAPPINESS

TODAY'S SCRIPTURE REFERENCE:

For the joy of the LORD is your strength.
Nehemiah 8:10 NIV

Today, I saw a bluebird, which made me smile. They are called the birds of happiness. There is even a song, "Bluebird of Happiness". The lyrics of the song talk about how life is filled with smiles and tears, as well as joy and fear. The chorus reminds the listeners to look for the "bluebird of happiness" or, in other words, the good in the bad and the light in the dark times.

Sad, isn't it? How close the world comes to the Truth, and yet, it is so very far away. The world sings about looking for the light, not knowing who the Light of the world is! Positive thinking and looking for good things in your life are good things to do, but they will not produce the lasting, true, blessed joy that peace with God brings.

In His sermon on the mountain found in Matthew chapter five, Jesus taught us how to truly be happy. He said that those who are humble in spirit, who see their need for Him, will not only be happy, but they will see the kingdom of heaven. Those who mourn over their sin shall be comforted with forgiveness and restoration of the relationship. Those who show restraint under persecution will receive blessings and inherit the earth. Jesus said that those showing mercy will be blessed by receiving mercy. Believers coming to Jesus to be made clean, holy, and pure will be happy and blessed to see God and be in a relationship with Him. True happiness is found only in Jesus, in our relationship with the Father through Him.

When I think about being happy, I also think about being content; I think these two things walk arm in arm. Paul referred to his contentment in Philippians. He said in Phil. 4:11-13 that he had learned to be content no matter what his circumstances might have been, whether in prison, in want, or in wealth. The secret of his contentment was finding his strength in Christ.

I can do all things through him who strengthens me.
Philippians 4:13 ESV

Paul had a living, breathing relationship with Christ, one in which he depended totally on Christ for everything in his life. He knew he was loved and that Jesus could meet his every need. Paul's secret was that he lived out Jesus' sermon. He knew he needed Jesus and humbled himself before Him. Paul mourned over sin. He sought after righteousness and mercy. Paul lived his life walking with Jesus, not chasing after a "bluebird of happiness." And Jesus made him happy. His Joy was his strength.

I cannot see a bluebird and not think of Glenn's mother, Cleo Acker, Granny, to her family. She loved bluebirds and had a collection of them around her house. For me, a bluebird does not represent the world's idea of happiness, but rather Paul's. Granny had a faith in Jesus like Paul's.

She lived a life of happiness, hope, and contentment because Jesus was her strength. She thirsted for Him and His righteousness. By resting in the completed work of Jesus, she showed her family how to pursue true happiness and contentment in this world.

PRAYERFUL RESPONSE:

Pray, asking our Father to place in you a desire to pursue Jesus. Ask for His guidance in your thoughts and actions as you seek to grow in your relationship with Jesus. Write a few things He revealed about finding contentment in your relationship with Him through Jesus.

_____

_____

_____

_____

_____

_____

_____

_____

PUT ON YOUR SHOES

TODAY'S SCRIPTURE REFERENCE:

*Let perseverance finish its work so that you may be mature
and complete, not lacking anything.*

James 1:4 NIV

Walking is part of my daily routine, and I usually love it. I often enjoy my surroundings and use walking as time with the Lord. But ugh—not on this particular day, because I was in a mood. My seasonal headache had been with me for two weeks and was wearing me down. Thank goodness it wasn't constant pain. I never know when it's coming or going.

So, I did not want to put on my shoes and hit the road. But surprisingly, I did. Despite my grumpy start, I began to enjoy the walk and increase my speed after the first half mile. The flowers were blooming, the trees were greening up, there was a lovely breeze, and my headache was disappearing!

God reminded me of the importance of putting on my walking shoes and going for a walk, even when I didn't want to. Then He went for the slam dunk and showed me that I should continue to walk in His Spirit, in my identity in Him, even when I didn't feel like it. The revelation stopped me dead in my tracks.

How many times have I let some circumstance, hurt feelings, or just plain stinking thinking rob me of remembering who I am in Jesus? I let the "shoes of my true identity" sit in my closet and try to walk out the Christian life on my own strength. But Jesus intended for us to walk in the freedom of His truth, as the gospel of John teaches:

> *You will know the truth, and the truth will set you free!*
> John 8:32 NIV

But what are we "free" to do? What are we "free" to be? In Galatians, Paul addresses our freedom as living in the Spirit and our identity in Christ. When we live in the Spirit, we love. And we bear the fruit of joy, peace, patience, kindness, goodness, faithfulness, gentleness, and self-control. As beloved children, we live under the reign of the King of Kings and Lord of Lords. By believing in our true identity as believers, He empowers us to act accordingly.

Putting on "the shoes of our identity" is paramount to us walking in the Spirit. Is it possible to practice something you don't believe you possess? In Jesus, God has already revealed our true identity.

As we step into our God-given "identity shoes," He helps us practice walking in them. He is there to teach us, encourage us, pick us up when we trip or fall, and help us get back on our feet. But He expects us to put them on, to believe that He is Who He says He is and that we are who He says we are!

Regardless of grumpy days full of doubts about love and forgiveness, keep walking in those shoes! You will discover, too, that this is the day the Lord has made, and you'll be able to rejoice and be glad in it (Psalm 118:24) because God is faithful and does not lie. You are complete in Christ!

PRAYERFUL RESPONSE:

Find these scriptures and note what they reveal about your true identity in Jesus. Remind yourself of your identity by reading these truths often and living out what you believe!

- John 1:12
- John 15:16
- Romans 5:1
- Romans 8:1
- Romans 8: 35-39
- 1 Corinthians 3:16
- 2 Corinthians 6:19-20
- Ephesians 1: 1-4
- Philippians 1:6
- 2 Timothy 1:7

_____

_____

_____

_____

_____

_____

_____

_____

REMINDERS

TODAY'S SCRIPTURE REFERENCE:

The LORD has helped us to this point.
1 Samuel 7:12 CSB

D o you need occasional reminders? Glenn and I have an inside joke between us. He'll ask me to remind him to do something, and then I'll ask, "Who's going to remind *me* to remind *you?*"!

We keep a calendar on the refrigerator to mark appointments and important dates such as birthdays and anniversaries. Then there are reminder lists, e.g., lists of chores to complete, groceries to purchase, etc. You get the idea; all of us need reminders!

What about spiritual reminders? I have self-diagnosed myself with "spiritual ADD"; my mind is prone to wander! I'm sure I'm not the only one. In 1st Samuel, we see where Samuel set up the stone of Ebenezer as a reminder to Israel that God routed the Philistines before them:

Thus far has the Lord helped us.
1 Samuel 7:12 NIV

Mezuzahs are placed on doorposts in traditional Jewish families to remind them of the oneness of God. When Glenn and I were in Israel, we bought one and put it on the doorpost of our front door.

Now, it reminds me to "love the Lord your God with all your heart and with all your soul and with all your might" (Deuteronomy 6:5 ESV).

Because of my wandering and forgetful mind, I have learned to place reminders around me—Ebenezer stones, if you will. I've strategically placed stones with the names of God around my house. Some are scripture cards taped to my mirror or computer screen. I keep an ongoing thankful list that keeps growing as He keeps blessing me.

Sometimes, especially during the dark days, we need to sit down with pen and paper and then recall the times when "thus far, the Lord has helped us." Because of our spiritual ADD, we tend to forget. However, our hope and faith are renewed when we do remember. We see where His hand moved in our past, giving us strength and confidence in the now.

I encourage you to place your reminders around you; keep them close by. Place them where you'll see them: in your Bible, journal, bedside, computer, mirror, or car. Ask the Holy Spirit to help you remember all the things He has done for you. It is a good thing to meditate on the "Ebenezer" times in our lives.

PRAYERFUL RESPONSE:

Make a list of promises of God that you want to remember. Pray, asking God to always keep these things in your mind! Ensure you note the times He has assisted you, as they are important to growing your faith.

_____

_____

_____

_____

_____

_____

_____

_____

SANCTUARY

TODAY'S SCRIPTURE REFERENCE:

*But let all who take refuge in you be glad; let them ever sing
for joy. Spread your protection over them, that those who
love your name may rejoice in you. For surely, O LORD, you
bless the righteous; you surround them with your favor as
with a shield.*

Psalm 5:11-12 NIV

The dictionary defines the word "sanctuary" as "a place of refuge or safety." A "refuge" is "a condition of being safe or sheltered from pursuit, danger, or trouble." When faced with stress, conflict, worry, confusion, and doubts, we all seek a sanctuary.

I live in what most people would call the perfect "sanctuary." As I walked the other day through beautiful woods with the lake around the bend, I thought how safe I felt from the world in my little sanctuary. Then, the Lord reminded me that I felt a sense of false security. As today's passage in Psalms tells us, He is the One who protects and shields us.

*God is our refuge and strength, an ever-present help in
trouble. Therefore, we will not fear, though the earth give
way and the mountains fall into the heart of the sea.*

Psalm 46:1-2 NIV

I thanked Him for reminding me of His role as my Protector, Shelter, Provision, and Sanctuary. What a relief! Because He is all these things for me, I can apply 1 Peter 5:6-7 and humbly cast all my anxiety and care on Him, knowing He loves me and will take care of me.

How priceless your faithful love is, God! People take refuge
in the shadow of your wings.
Psalm 36:7 CSB

Not only is He my refuge (sanctuary), but as a believer, the Holy Spirit dwells within me, making me His temple (1 Corinthians 3:16). As His spiritual temple, we are living stones being built into a spiritual house to be a holy priesthood, offering spiritual sacrifices acceptable to God through Jesus Christ (1 Peter 2:5).

Peter continues in that chapter, saying that we, as living stones, are to follow the example of Jesus and remember that we are strangers in this world. As aliens, we conduct ourselves honorably, thus bringing glory to God. Peter reminds us that it is God's will that we silence the ignorance of foolish people by doing good! Thankfully, the Holy Spirit within us enables us to do so!

How precious is our God? He is our Sanctuary. And yet, He makes *us* into sanctuaries of His Spirit to spread His love to a world that desperately needs Him. Our hearts' sanctuaries must worship and express gratitude towards him.

Lord, prepare me to be a sanctuary
Pure and holy, tried and true.
With thanksgiving,
I'll be a living Sanctuary for You.
JOHN THOMPSON, RANDY SCRUGGS

PRAYERFUL RESPONSE:

In what way is God your sanctuary? How do you live as the sanctuary of His Spirit?

_____

_____

_____

_____

_____

_____

_____

_____

_____

SHOES

TODAY'S SCRIPTURE REFERENCE:

*Stand, therefore, with truth like a belt around your waist,
righteousness like armor on your chest, and your feet
sandaled with readiness for the gospel of peace.*
Ephesians 6:14-15 CSB

I'm so excited because I got a new pair of walking shoes! The old ones were worn on the bottom, especially the right shoe. Always put your best foot forward! Ha! Anyway, the new ones are so much lighter and have more cushion, so it feels like I am walking on air. I can't wait to rack up the miles on them.

As I walked this morning, I pondered on the idea that God has gifted us all with a pair of spiritual shoes called gospel shoes. My mind meandered around the concept of walking in those shoes as my feet did the same down our country lanes. The gospel shoes are included in the armor of God and should be worn daily (Ephesians 6:10-17). We should mentally and consciously put them on every morning as we prepare for the day.

These shoes are known as "the gospel of peace." Another word for gospel is "Good News." And it is good news that we have peace with God through the blood sacrifice of Jesus Christ!

For in him all the fullness of God was pleased to dwell, and
through him to reconcile to himself all things, whether on
earth or in heaven,
making peace by the blood of his cross.
Colossians 1:19-20 ESV

The implications of this truth are astounding! We, as believers, walk, live, and breathe in the freedom of having peace with God. That freedom allows us to be at peace with others, too, because peace is a fruit of the Spirit (Galatians 5:22).

Here's the catch. God gives you these beautiful shoes, but you must put them on your stinky feet! Notice Paul says, "*Put on* the full armor of God." When you put on your gospel shoes of the good news, signifying that you are reconciled to God FOREVER, you can STAND YOUR GROUND against the lies of Satan. Additionally, you now hold the position of a messenger for Christ, tasked with the important duty of promoting unity (2 Corinthians 5:18-20 CSB).

Everything is from God, who has reconciled us to Himself through Christ and has given us the ministry of reconciliation. In Christ, God was reconciling the world to Himself, not counting their trespasses against them, and He has committed the message of reconciliation to us. Therefore, we are ambassadors for Christ, since God is making His appeal through us. We plead on Christ's behalf, "Be reconciled to God."

You walk in the Spirit, reconciled to God, having His peace. And in that peace, you can now tell others that they can have a pair of gospel shoes just like yours!

Cinderella showed us that putting on a new pair of shoes can change your life. But her shoes were made of glass, which can chip, crack, or break—either way, they can cut your foot! Yet, our generous Father equips us with custom-made shoes that are beyond measure.

We all have many pairs of shoes in our closets, some more than others. But when you get dressed in the morning, do you put on your best shoes so you can put your best foot forward?

PRAYERFUL RESPONSE:

Do you wear your gospel shoes every morning or keep them in your closet? Why is it essential for you to put them on daily?

_____

_____

_____

_____

_____

_____

_____

SIBLINGS

TODAY'S SCRIPTURE REFERENCE:

For he himself is our peace, who has made us both one and
has broken down in his flesh
the dividing wall of hostility.

Ephesians 2:14 ESV

How many mothers among you have experienced sibling rivalry? I dare say that if you have more than one child, it's a given! We raised three rambunctious boys who were always fighting, or at least it felt that way to us.

At one point, Glenn and I enrolled them in karate lessons. We thought it would teach them self-control and discipline, allowing them a safe place to release their energy. However, they thought it was super cool to wear white pajamas, yell, "Hy-yah," and play like the Karate Kid!

Here is what I observed about sibling rivalry. They may have fought with each other, but they had and have a deep love for one another. There was an unspoken code. They could pick on each other, but if anybody picked on one of the Acker boys, they picked on all three. Our boys had each other's backs because they loved each other.

No further explanation can account for the bond that was and still is. It can be weakened but not broken because it is not only a brotherly love but also an agape love found in Christ.

It is the same with the Body of Christ. In John 17, Jesus prays for His Body to be unified in this special bond of love with Him, the Father, and His Spirit. It is the mystery of the gospel. In John 17:23 NIV, He prays, "that they may be brought to complete unity. Then the world may know that You sent Me and have loved them even as You have loved Me".

Currently, our world is divided by many arguments, hostile opinions, divisions, debates, and contentions. The turmoil has caught up believers, with some finding themselves on opposing sides of the debate. We find ourselves involved in some "sibling rivalry," if you will.

How are we to respond to one another? The Bible is very clear: we are to love one another as the Father loves the Son, and the Son loves the Father. We are of the same Spirit.

In Ephesians, Paul addresses a huge contention between the early Christians: circumcision. He described it as the "dividing wall of hostility" between the brothers and sisters. But Paul explained to the Ephesians that:

> He [Jesus] might create in himself one new man in place of
> the two, so making peace, and might reconcile us both to
> God in one body through the cross, thereby killing the
> hostility. And he came and preached peace to you who were
> far off and peace to those who were near.
> Ephesians 2:15-16 ESV [Emphasis added]

Of course, Paul is explaining why circumcision is unnecessary. But he also shows that Jesus is our common denominator for reconciliation and peace, especially when there are walls of conflict and animosity among brothers and sisters in Christ.

The world must see us interact and react to one another with love, compassion, kindness, gentleness, and patience. The Biblical meaning for gentleness is to show restraint and self-control. Patience literally means long-tempered; it conveys the idea of a hesitancy to retaliate when wronged.

And why do we need to behave this way? The first answer that comes to my mind is because He said so! But seriously, we need to behave this way to exalt and glorify Jesus, honor God, and save the world!

As brothers and sisters in the Lord, we will not always agree or even like each other. But we are called to love, encourage, and have each other's backs. By demonstrating the love of Jesus to one another, we can reveal Jesus to the world through our actions. If not, we will draw them away from our Savior to our shame.

PRAYERFUL RESPONSE:

Are there "siblings" in your church family that you are contentious with? If not, do you know of members in your congregation who are? Pray for them, seeking God's guidance to understand their needs and hurts, as well as how to love them through your words and actions.

THE SPARROW

TODAY'S SCRIPTURE REFERENCE:

But You are holy, enthroned on the praises of Israel. Our fathers trusted in You; they trusted, and You rescued them. They cried to You and were set free; they trusted in You and were not disgraced.

Psalm 22:3-5 HCSB

I have this cute bird feeder that looks like a church house. It is relatively large, holding lots of birdseed. While setting it on the ground to refill it one morning, I heard a clamoring noise. Trapped inside the feeder was a sparrow! I have no idea how that little stinker managed to get himself in such a predicament.

I removed the roof of the feeder to allow him to escape, but he couldn't find an exit. He was panicky and disoriented, frantically flapping his wings against the inside of the feeder. With gloves on, I gently cupped my hands and lifted him up. Away he flew as soon as he realized he was above the sides of his prison!

After filling the feeder and putting the birdseed container back in the shed, I walked around the yard, taking pictures of the beautiful scenery all around with my phone. While approaching the birdfeeder to get pictures, a little sparrow flew straight at me, right up to my chest. He landed on my cell phone, tipped his wings at me as if to say, "Thank you," and then flew away! I won't be convinced otherwise - the same little sparrow I rescued earlier definitely flew straight at me!

The years dealing with Covid, and afterward with its continued challenges, have taught me the importance of having a thankful heart. Unquestionably, it keeps life in the proper perspective. We must keep our thoughts focused on what we do *have* rather than what we *do not*. And we must remember all the "prisons" that we need rescuing from. Undoubtedly, we need to remember to have a Rescuer.

Our hearts stay thankful when we focus on our blessings and our good Father who provides them. Moreover, it urges us to reflect on the truth, bolstering our faith. Our relationship with our Father grows through thankfulness. Thankfulness is key.

The lesson of the sparrow is important. Thankfulness leads to praise, which is the spark plug for our faith. God inhabits the praises of His people.

Rescued. Set free like the sparrow. Meditate on that. See if a thankful heart is not the result!

PRAYERFUL RESPONSE:

Write 20 things that bring you gratitude. Spend a few moments thanking your Good Father for His blessings. (Remember to include rescuing you from a life of sin and destruction!)

_____

_____

_____

_____

SPECIAL MOMENTS

TODAY'S SCRIPTURE REFERENCE:

You will seek me and find me,
when you seek me with all your heart.
Jeremiah 29:13 ESV

A few years back, we hosted our grandkids for a week: three twelve-year-olds, one ten-year-old, an eight-year-old, and one rough-and-tumble two-year-old. It was chaotic with blowup beds and toys and doors constantly opening and closing (*my floor will never be clean again*). I played the roles of playmate, short-order cook, housecleaner, wife, mother, and mother-in-law. Whew! What a glorious time we had!

We made special memories together, celebrating family, fun, and our love for each other. One thing I cherish most is the one-on-one times I had with each kid: throwing rocks in the water with Baxley, walking with Zoe and Khloe, riding the golf cart with Abigail and Seth, and my teaching time with Liam. (I helped homeschool him in language arts.) In these individual times with each kid, I got to know them better, and they got to feel a special bond with me.

That is what God desires with us. He wants to spend individual time with us so we can get to know Him and enjoy a special bond. We do that through prayer. As we sit with Him, abiding in His love through Jesus, and focus on the truths of His Word, we begin to communicate with Him the desires of our hearts.

He is a good listener who desires what is good for us because He is good. As we approach our Holy Father, we submit our wills to His, willing to listen to Him, too! That is what abiding means: to make ourselves at home with Him and His will. When we do that, our desires align with His, and we naturally pray within His will, praying that His will be done, and His Kingdom come.

Communication is the key to enhancing any relationship. Why would we neglect the most important relationship with our heavenly Father through His Son, Jesus? I encourage you to follow Paul's instructions in 1 Thessalonians 5:17-18 when he said to pray constantly and to give thanks in everything, for this is God's will. Remember that He is always with you, in you, "the Hope of Glory"! He is only a breath, a word away. Just speak His name; He will hear.

Rejoice always, pray without ceasing, give thanks in all
circumstances; for this is the will of God
in Christ Jesus for you.
1Thessalonians 5:16-18 ESV

PRAYERFUL RESPONSE:

Spend time with Him now in prayer, thankfully remembering His great love for you and desire for your good.

_____

_____

_____

_____

_____

_____

_____

_____

STAYING CONNECTED

TODAY'S SCRIPTURE REFERENCE:

After this manner therefore pray ye: Our Father which art in heaven, Hallowed be thy name. Thy kingdom come, Thy will be done in earth, as it is in heaven. Give us this day our daily bread. And forgive us our debts as we forgive our debtors. And lead us not into temptation, but deliver us from evil: For thine is the kingdom, and the power, and the glory, forever. Amen.

Matthew 6:9-13 KJV

When my grandson, Liam, was homeschooled, I helped supplement his language lessons twice a week. His then two-year-old brother, Baxley, frequently entered the room during the lesson. Oh, how it warmed my heart as I saw Bax's eyes light up when he saw me on the screen, and he would approach the computer to talk to me. Technology is a wonderful way to keep people who love each other connected, especially when they live hundreds of miles apart.

Prayer is like that; it is an incredible gift designed by God to keep us connected to Him. Our Abba Father in heaven loves us dearly, calls us His beloved children, and bestows upon us this blessing of prayer.

Every good and perfect gift is from above,
coming down from the Father of lights,
who does not change like shifting shadows.
James 1:17 CSB

When Jesus taught the wonderful Sermon on the Mount, His disciples asked Him to teach them to pray. While teaching them about the Kingdom of God and how to live within it, He stopped to give them the model prayer, what we now refer to as "The Lord's Prayer" (Matthew 6:6-13). The disciples had often observed Him in intimate conversations with His Father and yearned for that same experience with God. They had a hunger to be taught.

What about you? Do you have a hunger to be taught? Do you have a desire to have intimate conversations with our Father that lead to a more intimate, trusting relationship with Him? If you analyze His model prayer sentence by sentence, you will uncover a prayer technique. It's not just a prayer to memorize and say by rote. Each line is significant; Jesus is teaching us how to pray.

He begins with worship and praise, acknowledging Who God is. Then He prays His allegiance to God and Him alone, praying for His kingdom to come into the hearts of men and women—both now and for the kingdom's ultimate glorious coming.

Next, He teaches us to depend on our Father for our daily provisions for ourselves and for others. He reminds us that we are debtors who need to ask for forgiveness. He instructs us to forgive others since we have received much forgiveness. Having confessed sin and asking for forgiveness, we next ask for protection from evil for ourselves and others. Finally, we end our prayer with more adoration, thankfulness, and praise. We acknowledge He is King of the World; He is the power and the glory forever!

Praise God from whom all blessings flow! It's amazing how He provides a way for us to communicate and be with Him, filling our hearts with His Spirit, confidence, trust, joy, rest, thankfulness, and peace. Jesus is a good teacher, isn't He?

PRAYERFUL RESPONSE:

Open your Bible to Matthew 6:9-13 and pray through each topic sentence:

- Praise Your Father for His holiness, goodness, sovereignty, power, love, etc.
- Embrace Him as the Lord and Sovereign of your life, seeking His support in remaining loyal to His Kingdom and praying for His Kingdom to impact non-believers' hearts.
- Ask Him to help you be totally submissive to His will. Pray for the earth to be filled with the knowledge of Him. Pray for family and friends to be submissive to His will, as well, and pray for the mind of Christ for yourself and others.
- Pray for daily provisions for yourself, loved ones, and those around you - physically, materially, emotionally, and spiritually. Ask Him to help you live in total dependence on Him, remembering that He is able to supply all our needs according to His riches in Christ Jesus. (Philippians 4:19)
- Confess and ask for forgiveness for sins, knowing He is faithful to forgive you (1 John 1:19). Remember He forgives you, and so, forgive those who have offended you. You cannot casually approach our holy God in prayer, thinking He will ignore your sin. Pray that your heart will be broken by what breaks His.

- Ask God to help you stay on guard and respond to trials, testing, and temptations by counting them all joy, knowing that they produce endurance, strengthen your faith, and make you complete in Jesus. (James 1:2-4) Ask Him to help you to put on the armor of God and to stand firm against evil.
- Thank and praise Him because He always leads us in triumph in Christ (2 Corinthians 2:14). To God be the glory forever and ever!

SUBMISSION: A BOUNDARY OF LOVE

TODAY'S SCRIPTURE REFERENCE:

*Adopt the same attitude as that of Christ Jesus, who,
existing in the form of God, did not consider equality with
God as something to be exploited. Instead he emptied
himself by assuming the form of a servant, taking on the
likeness of humanity. And when he had come as a man, he
humbled himself by becoming obedient to the point of death,
even to death on a cross.*

Philippians 2:5-8 CSB

Before we delve into the "dreaded" topic of submission, let's witness it in action. Acts 4:1-20 depicts Peter and John standing before the rulers, elders, scribes, Annas, the high priest, Caiaphas, and the entire high priestly family. Peter and John have been in custody overnight because they healed a man who had been lame since birth. The religious rulers want to know how this man was healed and in whose name.

Peter, filled with the Holy Spirit, tells them that the man was healed by the name of Jesus, whom they crucified and whom God raised from the dead. Verse 13 (CSB) says, "When they observed the boldness of Peter and John and realized that they were uneducated and untrained men, they were amazed and recognized that they had been with Jesus." The authorities ordered Peter and John to speak no more in this name. But Peter and John answered, "Whether it's right in the sight of God for us to listen to you rather than to God, you decide, for we are unable to stop speaking about what we have seen and heard."

Two things leaped out at me in this passage: The rulers recognized that Peter and John had been with Jesus, and Peter and John had a boldness to speak because of their submission to Jesus and to His gospel. Jesus informed His Disciples that they would need to forsake themselves in order to follow Him (Mark 8:34). Submission is not just a concept; it is something we must do daily.

The rulers realized that Peter and John had been in the company of Jesus only after they spoke about Him and showed their dedication to His message and mission. They saw Jesus in Peter and John. And goodness—that's the way it's supposed to happen!

Submission is acknowledging that the Lord has authority over us. It's clear that it involves us surrendering our desires for His. By submitting to Him and His Word and living out its truths, people will recognize Jesus within us.

God's Word sets boundaries for how we submit to Him and to one another. When we submit to these boundaries, we let His words fill our hearts and minds so that our lives reflect the teachings of those scriptures. (Nick Acker, *Fully Forming*)

Titus 2:9-10 talks about how slaves are to interact with their masters, but we, too, are bondservants of the Most High God! Paul urges them to be submissive to their own masters in everything so that their behavior makes attractive the teaching of God and our Savior in everything and in every way.

When Jesus asked His Disciples, which includes you and me, to die to self, take up our cross, and follow Him, He did not ask us to do anything that He did not do Himself. He is our perfect example of submission as He submitted Himself to the will of the Father (Philippians 2). When we walk in submission to Him and to His Word, we make Jesus look beautiful and attractive to unbelievers and set an example for believers. Submission to our Savior shows the pure love of God to others.

PRAYERFUL RESPONSE:

What is your opinion on why submission is often viewed negatively? What does scripture teach us about submission? In what areas have you failed to submit to God's will? Ask Him to help you.

_____

_____

_____

_____

_____

_____

_____

_____

THERE'S HOPE IN THE GARDEN

TODAY'S SCRIPTURE REFERENCE:

*For we are his workmanship, created in Christ Jesus for good
works, which God prepared beforehand,
that we should walk in them.*

Ephesians 2:10 ESV

Weeds are so pesky; they try my soul! I keep pulling and pulling and make progress in one specific area. Then I look up, and another patch of them has sprung up in another spot of the garden!

But you know what I have noticed? The beauty of the garden's colors and brilliance overshadows the presence of weeds when viewed as a whole. The varieties of flowers, with their regal beauty, diverse shapes and forms, and beckoning hues, remind you of our Creator's creative power, imagination, and love. Thinking about His creative genius gives you joy and hope. Naturally, such a display commands your awe and appreciation.

The Spirit of Christ works in this way for us. We are to work on pulling those weeds in our spiritual gardens. But, in the meantime, we are yielding to Him. And as we do, He is sowing the seeds of joy, patience, goodness, kindness, compassion, self-control, gentleness, and peace in the gardens of our hearts.

For through the Spirit, by faith,
We ourselves eagerly wait for the hope of righteousness.
Galatians 5:5 ESV

As the Spirit produces His fruit—His flower garden—within us, our lives are being displayed for Christ. His beauty shines through us, attracting others to His beauty. Now, I know most of us have messy flower gardens! But that is the beauty of our Savior, you see. When we allow Him to grow His "flowers" in our gardens, they far outshine our weeds. And think how much more lovely our gardens will become as we continually work at pulling those weeds, one by one, as the Master Gardener points them out to us.

It is God who works in you, both to will
and to work for his good pleasure.
Philippians 2:13 ESV

This verse gives me great hope for my garden! God gives me the desire and the will to have a beautiful garden for Him. Additionally, as I work in my garden, He works in, with, and through me. I can rely on His gardening skills, power, wisdom, and guidance as I work and create my own unique garden that He—as the Master Gardener—has designed for me.

Do you know that He has one for you, too? He has master-planned gardens designed uniquely for each of us. Think of it, all of us, uniquely designed by God to be beautifully, aromatically displaying His love, goodness, grace, mercy, joy, kindness, and hope to the world! He knows we're "messy," but He has that covered with Jesus. I told you there was Hope in the garden!

PRAYERFUL RESPONSE:

What kind of "garden" do you desire for your life? How can you work with the Master Gardener to make your garden more lovely?

_____

_____

_____

_____

_____

_____

_____

_____

TOO GOOD TO BE TRUE

TODAY'S SCRIPTURE REFERENCE:

Praise the LORD, my soul; all my inmost being, praise his
holy name. Praise the LORD, my soul,
and forget not all His benefits.

Psalm 103:1-2 NIV

Have you ever received some news that was so wonderful that you thought to yourself, "This is too good to be true!"? Maybe some money came in that you weren't expecting, enabling you to pay a bill that was due. It could have been relief and joy from a clean scan after a cancer scare. For some of you, it might be the long-awaited news that you would have a baby. Whatever it was, we have all experienced that feeling of euphoria, excitement, and thankfulness that comes with an incredible blessing.

The Gospel is that kind of Good News: too good to be true, and yet, it is! Galatians 2:16 HCSB says, "No one is justified by works of the law but by faith in Jesus Christ." To be justified means to be declared righteous as if we never sinned. The Good News is a complex doctrine for many of us to accept emotionally; we feel it is too good to be true! We struggle with feeling like we still need to do something! But our justification is based solely on what Jesus has done for us. It is by grace alone that we are saved (Ephesians 2:5).

But the Gospel can be nothing less than *Too Good to be True* because that is who our God is: 100% Goodness. Psalm 107:1 (HCSB) says, "Give thanks to the LORD, for He is good; His faithful love endures forever."

In *What Is the Gospel,* Bryan Chapell gives an example of a drowning swimmer to explain biblical faith. He says to imagine a swimmer who has been rescued from drowning. The swimmer who was saved is now confidently walking along the beach, proudly declaring his survival because he had the foresight to call for help from the lifeguard!

Chapell goes on to say, "To understand biblical faith, we must think of ourselves as entirely exhausted from trying to survive spiritually and relying entirely on the strength of the lifeguard (Jesus) to save us. Our hope cannot be based on the strength of our faith—the wave of weakness and doubt are far too strong for that— but rather on Jesus' provision alone." What a relief to know that our faith is not in our faith. That is good news, which is absolutely "Too good," *and* "True!"

PRAYERFUL RESPONSE:

Spend some time writing a prayer to God, thanking Him for the news that is too good to be true! What are you doing to share this Good News with others?

_____

_____

_____

_____

_____

_____

_____

_____

_____

A TRUE STORY

TODAY'S SCRIPTURE REFERENCE:

*And we know that in all things God works for the good of
those who love him, who have been called
according to his purpose.*

Romans 8:28 NIV

Allow me to tell you a story of love. Just a few days before Christmas 2020, my daughter-in-law, Catherine, my grandkids, Seth and Abigail, along with Catherine's parents, were displaced by a fire in their home. They stayed with us for a few days before the insurance company placed them in a hotel close to Catherine's work.

Then, on Christmas Eve, someone broke into their trailer parked in the hotel parking lot and stole their Christmas gifts! What happened next can only be described as a Christmas miracle—acts of love by family, friends, and strangers.

For example, the hotel manager put the situation on his Facebook page, collected money and gift cards, and presented them to the family. Church friends and family scrambled to shop in every store they could find to replace the "Santa" gifts that were taken: a bicycle, bow and arrows, punching bag, dinosaurs, and clothes. Seth's best friend spent his own money buying one of Seth's gifts.

At first, Abigail and Seth were devastated. They could not believe someone would do something so cruel. Abigail said, "Who would be so mean to take children's presents on Christmas Eve?" But then, as they watched the kindness and generosity of people, they learned a valuable lesson.

Their family experienced firsthand the sacrifice of others on their behalf. They watched others give their time, effort, and money for them. In all this, they witnessed the true meaning of Christmas. After all they had been through, they experienced the truth that God is good. He can take what others mean for evil and make it into something better than presents. They are now aware of the deep love they have from their Heavenly Father and loved ones.

What a valuable lesson for each of us right now. No matter what situation we find ourselves in, one thing is constant: His love for us. His faithful love endures forever, and He will never leave or forsake us. He is for us, not against us. Moreover, He is always working for our good.

Ask my grandkids; they have been through a lot. Nevertheless, they are aware from personal experience that God is good and loves His children.

PRAYERFUL RESPONSE:

In what ways do you show the love of Jesus to others? How has God shown His love for you through the actions of others?

_____

_____

_____

_____

_____

_____

_____

_____

_____

TURN YOUR EYES
UPON JESUS

TODAY'S SCRIPTURE REFERENCE:

To you I lift up my eyes,
O you who are enthroned in the heavens!
Psalm 123:1 ESV

Helen H. Lemmel immigrated from England to America as a child. The daughter of a Wesleyan minister, she was a gifted songwriter, musician, and singer. She eventually returned to Europe to study vocal music in Germany, where she met and married a wealthy European man. Together, they moved back to America, where she became the vocal music teacher at the Moody Bible Institute. Sadly, when she went blind, her husband abandoned her.

At age 55, Helen heard a statement on a gospel tract that deeply moved her: "So then, turn your eyes upon Him, look full into His face, and you will find that the things of earth will acquire a strange new dimness."

Lemmel later said, "Suddenly, as if commanded to stop and listen, I stood still, and singing in my soul and spirit was the chorus of the hymn with not one conscious moment of putting word to word to make rhyme or note to note to make melody. The verses were written the same week, after the usual manner of composition, but nonetheless dictated by the Holy Spirit."

From this experience came the hymn we know as *Turn Your Eyes Upon Jesus*. It has a deeper meaning now for me knowing about the circumstances of the writer. I cannot sing it without tears filling my eyes as I imagine myself looking into Jesus' eyes.

O soul, are you weary and troubled?

No light in the darkness you see?

There's light for a look at the Savior,

and life more abundant and free!

Turn your eyes upon Jesus; Look full in His wonderful Face.

And the things of earth will grow strangely dim

In the light of His glory and grace.

HELEN HOWARTH LEMMEL

What are your eyes fixed upon? What are your thoughts constantly circling around? If they are fixed upon your circumstances, you will be tempted to waiver in your faith. You will worry yourself into a box of doubt and uncertainty. By focusing on the Author and Perfecter of your faith, you can experience peace and security amid doubts, uncertainties, and problems.

We must learn to battle through our moods, feelings, and emotions with absolute devotion to Jesus, remembering that He presents us faultless before the throne of God. He redeems us and is sanctifying us, making us righteous before the Father. He is sovereign and orchestrating everything for our benefit. Remember that your faith is not in your faith; your faith is in Jesus. Look full in His wonderful face!

PRAYERFUL RESPONSE:

In what way does focusing on Jesus strengthen your faith?

_____

_____

_____

_____

_____

_____

_____

_____

UNEXPECTED GIFTS

TODAY'S SCRIPTURE REFERENCE:

*Blessed is the God and Father of our Lord Jesus Christ, who
has blessed us with every
spiritual blessing in the heavens in Christ.*

Ephesians 1:3 CSB

In my front flower bed is a beautiful stand of flowers that I did not plant. At first, they appeared as blades resembling grass, but I could tell it was more than just grass. So, I decided to let them grow and see what happens. I watched it for a couple of years! Then, one day, I noticed a stem had grown with buds and before long, there stood this gorgeous wild fuchsia gladiolus—what an unexpected gift of beauty!

Whenever I walk by, it reminds me of the unexpected presents God gives upon us. In the book of James, we are told that every good and perfect gift comes from the Father. After reading this, I began to ponder the thought of unexpected gifts:

- ✓ a beautiful sunrise or sunset
- ✓ a chance encounter with a good friend
- ✓ a meal paid for by a stranger or friend
- ✓ an encouraging word at just the right time

I came to understand that with our God, there are no unexpected gifts. Jesus said that even we as sinners know how to give good gifts to our children, so how much more does our Father know how to give good gifts to those who ask Him (Matthew 7:11-12)!

John tells us that God's love for us is so great that even in our sin, He lavished His love on us through the death of His Son and made us His children. Jeremiah tells us He loves us with an everlasting love and draws us to Himself with lovingkindness (Jeremiah 31:3). God loves us like no other ever could. Therefore, we can *expect* good gifts from Him.

Ephesians reveals that God has generously given us every spiritual blessing through Christ. He has given us redemption through His blood and forgiveness of sins according to the riches of His grace, of which there is an endless supply. He has given us His Spirit, which empowers us to walk in a manner worthy of our calling, giving us wisdom and guidance. In Galatians, Paul points out that His Spirit gives us joy, peace, patience, kindness, goodness, gentleness, and self-control. What wonderful gifts He gives to us! Paul encourages us to stay in step with the Spirit, walking in these gifts that He freely gives us.

I pray that we will always be thankful for all God's gifts. We should never take them for granted or see them as "unexpected" because He is a Good Father. He gives us exactly what we need, precisely when we need it.

PRAYERFUL RESPONSE:

Which gifts of God have been unexpected? What gifts have you taken for granted? Meditate on His goodness.

_____

_____

_____

_____

_____

_____

_____

_____

_____

UNWAVERING FAITH

TODAY'S SCRIPTURE REFERENCE:

Now faith is the assurance of things hoped for, the conviction of things not seen. For by it, the people of old received their commendation.

Hebrews 11:1-2 ESV

I have always identified with the Father who cried out to Jesus, "I believe; help my unbelief" (Mark 9:24 ESV). Wrestling with doubt and questions has caused me to lose sight of what I know to be true. Thank God for His precious Holy Spirit and the power of the Truth of His written Word, because I have learned how to apply His truth and replace whatever lie I have been thinking with God's words. I know God is a Promise Maker and a Promise Keeper.

Faith is the assurance of things hoped for, the conviction of things not seen.

Hebrews 11:1

It is the confidence that God is Who He says He is and He will do what He says He will do. The Ryrie Study Bible ASV commentary says, "Biblical faith is not some vague hope grounded in wishful thinking, but a settled confidence in the promises of an eternal, all-powerful, faithful, wise God . . . Who revealed Himself in His word and in the person of Jesus Christ." Biblical faith is grounded in the reality of Christ's death, burial, and resurrection.

Our faith affects everything we do, so let us remember some gifts we have BY FAITH:

- We have access to God with Jesus as our mediator (Hebrews 8:1-7).
- We walk with Him and have forgiveness. (Hebrews 8:8-12.
- We have the Holy Spirit. (Luke 11:13; John 14:26).
- We are protected and have victory in the world and over Satan; we are more than conquerors! (Romans 8:37).
- We can endure trials and hard circumstances. (James 1:2-4; 1 Peter 1:6-9).

God always answers us in accordance with His plan, purpose, kindness, goodness, and loving-kindness at the perfect time for our benefit and His glory to His glorious name. But, for us to deal with our wavering faith, there are some things we can do.

First, recognize the things that cause you to waver! Human reason conflicts with God; His ways are not our ways! Second, we allow our feelings to override our faith. Third, we fail to see God in our circumstances, at least not at first! Remember, He is most interested in transforming us into the image of Christ.

Fourth, we waver when we listen to unwise counsel; be careful who you listen to. Fifth, it is easier to waver in our faith when we focus on our situation rather than God and His purposes. Sixth, we waver when ignorant of His ways; we must know what scripture says for ourselves! Last, we waver when we hold on to guilt for something He has already forgiven. We need to let go of groundless guilt and rest in the freedom and blessings of His love and forgiveness!

Wavering faith has yucky consequences. James calls a person of wavering faith "double-minded" or wishy-washy and unstable in all their ways. People with wavering faith lose their joy and their influence. They miss out on the blessings of God and make wrong, costly decisions, thus losing peace in their lives.

I remember an old Amy Grant song titled "I Have Decided" that describes biblical faith. It's about deciding to believe God unwaveringly. Now, do I succeed at this 100% of the time? Of course not!

But I am better; I am learning. I am a work in progress. He is growing me, and I am so grateful for His long suffering! Oh, how precious is His *faithfulness*, even in our *faithlessness*.

> I have decided,
> I'm gonna live like a believer.
> Turn my back on the deceiver,
> I'm gonna live what I believe.
> MICHAEL CARD

PRAYERFUL RESPONSE:

Think about a time when your faith wavered. What were your thoughts? Which of the seven ways listed in the devotional do you primarily tend to waver in? What can you do to increase your faith rather than waver?

_____

_____

_____

_____

_____

_____

_____

_____

WAIT

TODAY'S SCRIPTURE REFERENCE:

For God alone my soul waits in silence; From him comes my
salvation. He alone is my rock and my salvation,
my fortress; I shall not be greatly shaken.
Psalm 62:1-2 ESV

As you've read by now, my trips to California fill me with precious memories and Baxley stories! One of the hardest lessons this little person has to learn from his mommy and daddy is to wait. He was born with zero patience; he wants their attention when he wants it, and he does not care if they are otherwise engaged! His favorite command is, "Come." If you do not come when he says come, well, let's say it isn't pretty.

Then his mom or dad says, "Uh oh! Looks like you need to go to your room. Do you want to go by yourself, or shall I take you?" Many times, you can hear his door shut in the next county; that's when you know he took himself.

Baxley's mom and dad have a plan. They are teaching him to put his hand on their arm when he wants to tell them something when they are busy talking to someone else. They then put their hand over his to let him know that they know he is there and will listen to him soon. It is a work in progress, like everything else with a two-year-old, but he is learning.

Just. Like. Us.

We were born with zero patience; we want what we want when we want it, too. We are works in progress, learning to trust the One who loved us with a Cross. Our Heavenly Father is gently and patiently teaching us to be still and wait on Him.

Commit your way to the LORD; trust in him, and he will act.
He will bring forth your righteousness as the light
and your justice as the noonday.
Psalm 37:5-6 ESV

Isaiah tells us that we who learn to wait on the Lord "shall renew their strength; they shall mount up with wings like eagles; they shall run and not be weary; they shall walk and not faint" (Isaiah 40:31 ESV).

I have a suggestion. As we follow the instructions of Psalm 37, commit our way to the Lord, and trust Him, let us practice waiting like Baxley. Let us place our hand on our Savior's arm and, in our Spirit, feel Him put His hand over ours. Then, let us wait beside Him as He renews our strength as promised in Isaiah! As He calms our hearts and minds, we can approach His "throne of grace, that we may receive mercy and find grace to help in time of need" (Hebrews 4:16 ESV). We can wait in His Presence, knowing He loves us, is with us, and is working for our good.

What a good, good Father we have! He knows just what we need. (Matt. 6:32)

One side note: for those parenting little ones (*and big ones!*), remember that while you are parenting, you are being parented! Interesting concept, is it not? As you think about this, I wonder if it could affect how you respond to your children or how you approach their misbehavior. There may be a wealth of wisdom to be *caught* while they are being *taught*! That could change your whole perspective and attitude, thus affecting theirs!

PRAYERFUL RESPONSE:

How is God teaching you to wait? How can you respond to Him while you wait?

_____

_____

_____

_____

_____

_____

_____

_____

THE WAITING GAME

TODAY'S SCRIPTURE REFERENCE:

*Be strong and courageous. Do not be afraid or
terrified because of them, for the LORD your God goes with
you; he will never leave you nor forsake you.*

Deuteronomy 31:6 NIV

I need to confess that I am not a patient person. However, I have learned some interesting aspects about patience over the years. I've become aware of my ability to be more patient with certain things and specific individuals.

I can be patient if I divert my attention from the situation that might cause impatience. Remembering the times when people were patient with me helps me be more patient.

Who is more patient with us than God Himself? Who is more "mindful that we are but dust?" Whose mercies are new every morning? Whose lovingkindness endures forever? Yet, so many of us are impatient with God, especially when He says, "Wait."

One of my "go-to" verses over my lifetime has been:

I believe that I shall look upon the goodness of the LORD in
the land of the living!
Wait for the LORD; be strong and let your heart take
courage; wait for the LORD!
Psalm 27:13-14 ESV

What a comfort these verses have been for me as I have waited! They have helped to instill hope and patience in my heart as I wait for Him to work out His plans and purposes.

You see, <u>wait</u> is not passive; it is an active verb! *Strong's Concordance* defines it as "to look for eagerly, to hope, to expect" and "to bind together for strength; to be strong and robust." Waiting involves binding myself to the Lord like a "twisted cord or rope," as I expect Him to act on my behalf!

Deuteronomy 31:6 tells us to be strong and courageous because God is with us and will never leave or forsake us! So, while we wait (eagerly looking forward to what He is going to do), we imagine ourselves tied to Him with a strong cord that cannot be broken! We strengthen our bond with Him during this time by staying in the Word, praying, being in fellowship with believers, listening to gospel music and sermons, and talking with close friends who keep us accountable to the Truth.

My impatience has taught me a valuable lesson: waiting is inevitable. There is no "arrival" or "end game." Life is a continuous journey of self-improvement, and we are His handiwork in Christ Jesus. He is constantly molding and shaping us into the image of His Son, and waiting is part of that process. Waiting is vital to our growth, maybe the most important part.

For many, it is the present; it is what you have now. Don't waste it whining and throwing yourself a pity party about what you think you don't have that you are missing out on. Just maybe the waiting is the treasure you seek!

PRAYERFUL RESPONSE:

Most likely, you are waiting on the Lord for something right now! Dedicate some time to discussing it with Him, writing down your desires and needs. As you record your concerns, seek His peace, patience, and presence.

_____

_____

_____

_____

_____

_____

_____

_____

WALK THIS WAY

TODAY'S SCRIPTURE REFERENCE:

But I say, walk by the Spirit, and you will not carry out the
desire of the flesh.
Galatians 5:16 NASB

E very day, I walk two to three miles, and we're fortunate to live in such a beautiful area for walking! Even though there is beauty all around me, there are hazards to be mindful of as I go down my oil roads. For example, the road is uneven, with small potholes and patches of gravel. It gets slippery after a rain with muddy spots. Next, drivers are not always careful and courteous as they drive by on our skinny road! Then there are the occasional snakes, but that is an entirely different story!

As I've read through Paul's epistles, I keep encountering a recurring theme—be careful how you walk. Of course, we must be mindful of uneven roads, patches of gravel, slippery messes, rude drivers, and snakes! But more importantly, we must be cautious as we navigate our lives in front of our families, friends, and the world.

We have been instructed to "walk" in a specific manner.

Walk by the Spirit, and you will not carry out
the desire of the flesh.
Galatians 5:16 NASB

The Greek word for "walk" is *peripateo*, which means to regulate one's life, to conduct oneself. Paul goes on in the rest of Galatians, chapter 5, to explain what a life regulated by the Spirit looks like. It is full of the fruit of the Spirit, including love, joy, peace, patience, kindness, goodness, faithfulness, gentleness, and self-control.

In Colossians 2:6, Paul says we are to walk in Jesus, being rooted and built up in Him and established in the faith. Then, in chapter three, he tells us what to avoid (hazards along the way!) and what to do. He uses pretty strong language by telling us to "put to death" what is earthly in us by setting our minds on Christ and things above!

To walk the "walk," we must put off anger, wrath, malice, slander, obscene talk, and lying. It is important for us to demonstrate compassionate hearts, kindness, humility, meekness, patience, forbearance, and forgiveness. He sums it all up by saying that everything we say or do is to be done in Jesus' name with thanksgiving!

Walking "this Way" takes steadfast prayer (Colossians 4:2) and wisdom, making the best use of the time we've been given (Colossians 4:5). In Ephesians, Paul cautions us to stay alert against deceit and to be wise in understanding the Lord's will. We are to give thanks always and for everything to God in Jesus' name and to submit to one another for His sake (Ephesians 5:1-20 NIV).

Then, in Thessalonians, Paul urges believers to walk and to please God "more and more," for this is the will of God, your sanctification. (1 Thessalonians 4:1-3) But before that, in chapter 2, he said, "You received the word of God . . . which is at work in you believers."

How precious is our Lord! He places His Spirit in us and then gives us His written word to work in us, transforming us, sanctifying us, making us new so that we can, in His strength and power, walk "This Way." Our part is to yield our way to His with humility, love, joy, and thankfulness...then to be alert, to guard our hearts by remembering who we were and who we are now in Christ, by being wise, being obedient, loving Him fiercely, loving and encouraging each other, and being continually grateful and full of praise!

There is one other Greek word that Paul used for "walk" as found in Galatians:

> Since we live by the Spirit, let us keep in step [walk/stoicheo] with the Spirit. Let us not become conceited, provoking one another, envying one another.
>
> Galatians 5:25-26 NIV [Emphasis added]

Paul uses a different word here to illustrate how we as believers are to "proceed in a row as the march of a soldier; stay in rank" with the Spirit. In my mind, I see us linking arms, walking "This Way" together, supporting each other, holding each other up, encouraging one another, keeping alert for our brothers and sisters, and hoping they are doing the same for us because we all have the same Spirit! The key is constantly being filled with compassionate hearts and thanksgiving.

If we belong to Jesus, we've been called to walk "This Way" and are on the road. Jesus walks beside us, guiding us with His Spirit and His Word. Let's link our arms, keep our eyes on Him and the road, stay alert, and walk "This Way" with thanksgiving and a skip in our step!

PRAYERFUL RESPONSE:

How can you keep alert to the "hazards" along the way as you walk with the Spirit? Walking (*stoicheo*) in step with the Spirit as in a rank and file is to be done individually with His Spirit and corporately with other believers in His Spirit. Seek the guidance of the Spirit to practice "stoicheo" with Him.

_____

_____

_____

_____

_____

_____

_____

_____

_____

WATCH OUT FOR SNAKES

TODAY'S SCRIPTURE REFERENCE:

*For our struggle is not against flesh and blood, but against
the rulers, against the authorities,
against the cosmic powers of this darkness,
against evil, spiritual forces in the heavens.*

Ephesians 6:12 CSB

As I finished my three-mile walk, I was about to slow down and walk back home when I suddenly felt a sharp sting on my ankle. I jumped up and landed a couple of feet ahead of where I was about to step. Looking back, I saw a cotton mouth coiled up in the road! And yes, he'd gotten me!

I immediately called Glenn, thinking he needed to bring his shotgun. He asked me if I was bleeding, and at first, I said "no." Then I noticed two spots of blood on my ankle about a half-inch apart. That's when I called Wes, our doctor son, who told me to go to the ER immediately!

To make a long story short, it was a dry bite, meaning the snake had not pumped any venom into my leg. Whew, God was watching over me! I'll never know if I jumped high and fast or if the snake saved his venom for a tastier dinner. Either way, I am thankful for the mercy and grace I received that day.

Here's the lesson I learned: watch out for snakes! It's sad because I'm already familiar with how to do this. This wasn't the first time I encountered a snake on our roads. In the past, I have walked around, leaped over, and gone in the opposite direction from snakes slithering across the road. So, what was different about this time? I wasn't focused because I was distracted by my phone.

> *Be sober-minded; Be alert. Your adversary*
> *the devil is prowling around like a roaring lion,*
> *looking for anyone he can devour.*
> 1 Peter 5:8 CSB

In the Ephesians, chapter 6, Paul teaches us that we must put on the whole armor of God to stand against the devil's tactics. The devil is a cunning trickster, fluent in the language of lies and deception. We must be prepared to stand against him and be aware of his nature.

Then, equipped with the Word of God, we can resist him. We can't do that if we're lollygagging down the road, not paying any attention to what's happening around us spiritually!

All of us are guilty of letting "life" distract us from the best things but also of not being watchful of the enemy, who most likely is the distracter! Satan does not have the power of God; he's not omnipresent or all-powerful.

So, he uses sleight-of-hand tricks to lure you away from God's best for you. He teases your pleasure needs, your need for attention, and the desire for control or thrills.

He twists the truth to make his lies sound pleasant or harmless. But don't be fooled! His sting hurts, and his venom is deadly. It destroys relationships (yours with God for a time), families, churches, testimonies, and influences for Christ.

Let's be vigilant and remind each other of these things: Put on your armor! Always persevere in prayer for everyone with thanksgiving! Stand firm in the Lord and in His gospel of peace.

Set your minds on things that are above,
not on things that are on earth.
Colossians 3:2 ESV

Submit to God. But resist the devil, and he will flee from you.
Draw near to God, and He will draw near to you. Cleanse
your hands, sinners, and purify your hearts, double-minded
people.
James 4:7-8 HCSB

Don't let your guard down; don't be distracted and watch out for snakes in the road!

PRAYERFUL RESPONSE:

You cannot put on the armor of God if you don't know what it is; nor can you discern lies from truth if you do not know the truth. What can you do to strengthen your faith and stand firm against your enemy, Satan? Pray, asking God for discernment, guidance, knowledge, and wisdom as you practice staying alert and standing firm in your faith.

_____

_____

_____

_____

_____

_____

_____

_____

WATCH OUT, HERE SHE COMES

TODAY'S SCRIPTURE REFERENCE:

Be on your guard; stand firm in the faith; be courageous; be strong. Do everything in love.

1 Corinthians 16:13-14 NIV

One morning, as I took off down our little tree-lined lane, I could hear the birds calling to one another, "Watch out! Here she comes!" Like I am any danger to them! But they don't know that, so they courageously call each other to take cover and stand guard over their loved ones. I laughed because it reminded me of three mischievous little boys who used to warn each other with the exact words for different reasons!

But then my thoughts went to all the warnings God gives us in His Word to watch out, guard against, take a stand, and plant our feet firmly upon the Rock of our salvation. Unlike the birds who have nothing to fear from me, we do have an enemy who is out to destroy us. Satan prowls around like a roaring lion, looking for someone to devour, but we can resist him by standing firm in our Faith. (1 Peter 5:8-9) God of all grace and glory strengthens us and empowers us to make us strong, firm, and steadfast! (5:10)

Our God is perfect. He tells us exactly what we need to stand against this enemy. In 1 Peter 5:6, He instructs us to submit ourselves to His authority, trusting Him to take care of all things in His goodness and timing. As we do that, His power and strength enable us to stand against all the lies the devil can throw at us. We step into our armor, one piece at a time, knowing it is God's suit!

I am a Marvel fan, and, in my imagination, I can see God's Armor flying onto me like Ironman's! Think how cool that would be! The belt of the truth of His Word—WHAP! The breastplate of Righteous—BOOM! The shoes of the gospel of peace—ZAP!

In addition to all this, we take up the shield of Faith, and then, here it comes, the helmet of Salvation—WHOOSH! Next, God hands us His Word as our Sword, our weapon to wield as Jesus did in the wilderness. As we cover our armor in prayer (Ephesians 6:18), we stay alert, ready to be strong in the Lord and the power of His might (Ephesians 6:10)!

What do we stand against? I believe we are to keep alert and watchful over ourselves because Satan uses us against ourselves! Left to our own devices, we gravitate toward self-centered living, opening ourselves up to all kinds of sin and temptations. And our enemy is waiting just around the corner.

We must be watchful about what we see, think about, read, do, and speak. We are to be watchful about how we spend our time. We are to guard our hearts against lies; the only way to do that is to know the truth of His Word.

And that means studying and meditating, feeding our spirits, and saying His words daily. We train and practice the spiritual disciplines: study, meditate, fast, serve, worship, pray, confess sin, submit, and celebrate Him. Each day, we clothe ourselves in His armor, aware that only through Him can we stand firm in the Faith He bestows upon us.

I find it interesting that Paul added the "loving" part in today's scripture verse. Don't you? It implies that we are not alone in standing guard. United in love, we don His armor, stand side by side, love and uphold each other, creating a formidable wall of Christ's Body to face our common adversary. Watch out, devil; here we come!

PRAYERFUL RESPONSE:

What are you doing to stand guard over your self-centeredness and pride? Pray, asking the Father to help you put on His armor daily.

_____

_____

_____

_____

_____

_____

_____

_____

_____

WE WILL NOT BE SHAKEN

TODAY'S SCRIPTURE REFERENCE:

For God alone, O my soul, wait in silence, for my hope is from him. He only is my rock and my salvation, my fortress; I shall not be shaken. On God rests my salvation and my glory; my mighty rock, my refuge is God. Trust in him at all times, O people; pour out your heart before him; God is a refuge for us.

Psalm 62:5-8 ESV

We live in a shakable world. One thing is certain: these times are uncertain. But we have an Unshakable God incapable of change; He cannot be moved. He is forever faithful, the same today, yesterday, and forever. He is who He says He is and will do what He says He will do.

Our God is trustworthy, keeping every promise in His Word. We find comfort and peace in this amazing attribute of God. Sometimes we feel like we are being knocked off our feet, but He is our sure foundation, our solid rock. He is the Hope that we cling to when everything else is shifting sand.

Psalm 62 gives us instructions on how to handle these challenging days. First, we are to wait in silence before God alone, not in our finances, loved ones, or schemes, but in the One who knows everything about the past, present, and future. In Hebrew, "wait" means to be still, to tarry, to be astonished! How are we to wait?

In silence and with expectation, knowing our hope comes from Him. Secondly, in verse six, we are reassured that as we wait, expecting God to act, knowing He is our Rock, our place of refuge and salvation, we will not be shaken by the circumstances that surround us!

Remember that we are Kingdom Seekers. His Kingdom will never be shaken. Our salvation is secure; nothing can ever separate us from Him in Christ Jesus. God is our refuge, our shelter, and our provision. Because He cannot be moved, He can always be trusted in all circumstances (Psalm 62:8). So, as we wait (tarry in His presence), we expect and hope, knowing He is our salvation and provision. We trust Him to be mighty on our behalf.

This verse gives us one more instruction: we are to pour out our souls before Him because He is our safe place. He is a good Father who wants us to discuss everything with Him like Jesus did. We stay in His presence, remembering Who our God is.

Because He is our Refuge, Hope, Rock, Salvation, and Fortress, we can pour out our heart's desires to him, expecting Him to work on our behalf and for our good and His glory. And we will not be shaken because we are in Him, and He is for us.

PRAYERFUL RESPONSE:

Have you been in or are currently in circumstances that shook you to the core of your beliefs? In what way can Psalm 62 provide strength during difficult times?

_____

_____

_____

_____

_____

_____

_____

_____

WHAT IS IT?

TODAY'S SCRIPTURE REFERENCE:

When the Israelites saw it, they asked one another, "What is it?" because they didn't know what it was. Moses told them, "It is the bread the LORD has given you to eat."
Exodus 16:15 CSB

"I am the bread of life," Jesus told them. "No one who comes to me will ever be hungry, and no one who believes in me will ever be thirsty again."
John 6:35 CSB

For 40 years in the wilderness, God provided just what His people needed to survive physically and spiritually. He gave them sweet water (turned the bitter, stagnant water into living, sweet water, as found in Exodus 115:22-27). Furthermore, He gave them sweet bread, manna, which appeared each morning for six days, with enough on the sixth to carry them through the Sabbath. He was teaching them He is their Provision; He was teaching them about His Grace.

Do you want to know God's will for your life? He plainly tells you in 1 Thessalonians 4:3; it is for your sanctification. His will for you is that you live a holy life, set apart for Him, loving Him with your actions of obedience and serving other people in love. And here's why we do that: Grace.

The more I study the Scriptures, the more astonished I am with Grace. Like the Israelites, I stand in awe and ask, "What is it?!" The standard answer is God's merciful kindness and favor towards us. But, in pouring over different passages, the scope of His kindness and favor is as big as our Almighty God! We won't comprehend all its implications until we come face to face with Him.

For the grace of God has appeared, bringing salvation for all people, training us to renounce ungodliness and worldly passions, and to live self-controlled, upright, and godly lives in the present age, waiting for our blessed hope, the appearing of the glory of our great God and Savior, Jesus Christ.
Titus 2:11-13 ESV

We see that grace turns our hearts toward Jesus, redeeming us, bringing us to salvation, and training us in godliness. As we learn to practice godliness, we can live upright lives for Him while we wait for His return. His grace is the foundation for all of God's commands and directives to us. Furthermore, His expectations are achievable thanks to His prior actions for and within us. The *Wiersbe Bible Commentary* says grace redeems, reforms, and rewards us!

God's grace is transforming grace. It teaches me how to live. It strengthens me and encourages me so that I can deny worldly living and live a self-controlled life by practicing righteous living. Grace also teaches me where to look and who to look to: Jesus, my Savior, Redeemer, Deliverer, Friend, Rescuer, and Blessed Hope.

Grace. What is it? I still cannot explain it. But I am forever grateful for it.

PRAYERFUL RESPONSE:

Write your own definition of God's grace. Make time to thank Him for it!

_____

_____

_____

_____

_____

_____

_____

WIND BENEATH MY WINGS

TODAY'S SCRIPTURE REFERENCE:

But the Advocate, the Holy Spirit, whom the Father will send
in my name, will teach you all things and will remind you of
everything I have said to you.
John 14:26 NIV

Bette Midler's Song, *Wind Beneath My Wings*, typically causes me to cry when I listen to it. That's because it makes me think of people who have encouraged me, stood by me, and helped me grow spiritually and emotionally. If you're not familiar, here are a few lines from the song:

> Did you ever know that you're my hero
> and everything I would like to be?
> I can fly higher than an eagle,
> for you are the wind beneath my wings.
>
> It might have appeared to go unnoticed,
> but I've got it all here in my heart.
> I want you to know I know the truth.
> Of course, I know it;
> I would be nothing without you.

You are the wind beneath my wings.
Fly. You let me fly so high.
Thank God for you, the wind beneath my wings.

As you read those lyrics, someone special probably came to mind. They could have been someone who loved you, taught you, supported you, or made you laugh and get over yourself.

Here's another thought about this song: Not all the words apply, of course, but the idea of being the wind beneath our wings makes me think of the Holy Spirit. Jesus called Him "another Counselor" who will be with us forever, the "Spirit of Truth" (John 14:16-17).

The Greek for counselor is *parakletos,* which means helper, to speak cheerfully to, to encourage. It refers to one who comes forward as an advocate on behalf of another. The Holy Spirit witnesses to Jesus and acts as His substitute on earth while Christ is away. He is our Counselor and Keeper. We are sealed by the Holy Spirit, forever God's child, with a guaranteed inheritance (Ephesians 1:13-14).

Did you know birds take off *into* the wind? They use the wind speed to generate sufficient lift to achieve a higher altitude in less time. Just think! Jesus told His disciples that before He ascended, they would receive power from the Holy Spirit, enabling them to be His witnesses, and they did, and they were (Acts 1)!

That same Spirit empowers us. The Holy Spirit, our teacher, reminds us of Jesus' words (John 14:26) to empower us to live fruitful lives and be powerful witnesses to His Life. We are the Temple of the Holy Spirit (1 Corinthians 3:16). He strengthens us with the same resurrection power thus, enabling us to be witnesses, live holy lives, and love as Christ loves. He is the wind beneath our wings. And because of that, we must be the wind beneath each other's wings. Christ dwells within us, making us one with Him. One Lord, one Spirit, one Body, united in the love of God.

PRAYERFUL RESPONSE:

Reflect on times when the Holy Spirit has been the "wind beneath your wings." In what ways are you the wind beneath someone's "wings"?

_____

_____

_____

_____

_____

_____

_____

_____

_____

YOUR OWN
PERSONAL PRAYER
BOOK

Years ago, when my boys were teenagers, I attended a women's retreat in Falls Creek, Oklahoma. The retreat's key speaker was Kay Arthur; undoubtedly, it was a life-changing experience. I started viewing my Bible as both God's words and my Prayer Book.

Kay Arthur and other women in the breakout sessions pointed out written prayers in the Word and encouraged us to pray them for the people in our lives. I know that may sound simplistic to you, but for me, it opened a whole new way to pray for my children! They also showed us how to pray other scripture over our loved ones.

When I arrived home, my excitement led me to search the scriptures, starting with the Old Testament, and compose 365 daily prayers for my sons. At first, I tried to get my prayers published; I have 21 rejection letters to prove it!

Now, I simply give them to women at conferences, retreats, or Bible studies. I want to share a few of them with you below, hoping you, too, will see your Bible as a storehouse of prayers for you and your family.

These Scriptures are taken from the New American Standard Version (NASB), and I encourage you to write your loved one's name in the blank as you pray these over them:

- May _____ delight in Your Word and meditate on it daily until it becomes a natural part of their thinking. (Psalm 1:2-4)

- Father, I pray that Jesus will come to have first place in everything in _____'s life. (Colossians 1:18)

- Turn _____'s eyes from vanity and make their ways Your ways. Establish Your Word in them as that which produces reverence for You. (Psalm 119:37-38)

- Father, give_____ a thankful heart! Help them to give thanks to You abundantly and to praise You for all to see. (Psalm 109:30)

- I pray that _____'s love grows in knowledge and discernment to discern the things that are excellent in order to be sincere and blameless so that they may be filled with the fruit of righteousness that comes from Jesus. (Philippians1:9-11)

- Construct a hedge to protect _____ from encountering the wrong individuals and locations. (Hosea 2:6)

- Help _____ to be strong in the Faith, giving glory to You, not wavering with doubt or unbelief. (Romans 4:20)

- Father, help_____ to hate sin and to diligently seek You for You have promised us that those who seek You will find You. (Proverbs 8:13,17)

I will close with the blessing Nick and Beka say over their children each night before they go to sleep:

The LORD bless you and keep you: the LORD make His face shine upon you and be gracious to you; the LORD lift up his countenance upon you and give you peace.
Numbers 6:24-26 ESV

Like me, I pray you will look at your Bible with fresh eyes to see God's wonderful Gift to us! He gives us His very own Words of Truth to pray in and over every situation! He truly is a Good and Gracious Father, full of faithful love and compassion!

PRAYERFUL RESPONSE:

Choose one of your favorite scriptures and turn it into a prayer for yourself and those you love.

How can a young man keep his way pure? By guarding it according to your word. With my whole heart I seek you; let me not wander from your commandments. I have stored up your word in my heart, that I might not sin against you. Blessed are you, O Lord; teach me Your statutes! With my lips I declare all the rules of Your mouth. In the way of your testimonies, I delight as much as in all riches. I will meditate on your precepts and fix my eyes on your ways. I will delight in your statutes; I will not forget your word!

Psalm 119:9-16 ESV

ABOUT THE AUTHOR

Author Linda Acker is a retired schoolteacher and counselor, having spent her career encouraging hundreds of young adults. For over 45 years, she has served in various capacities within the local church: Sunday School teacher, Women's Ministry leader, Bible Study teacher, and Retreat speaker.

She and her husband, Glenn, have been married for 53 years and are the proud grandparents of ten grandkids! When she's not involved in church work, you'll find Linda working in her beautiful yard, taking walks along their lakeside home, or spoiling her grandchildren with lots of love.

Linda's deep desire is to encourage people to find the Lord in the everyday occurrences and experiences of life.

Made in the USA
Columbia, SC
07 March 2024